# Cyberterrorism

The world today is becoming more interconnected than ever before. Because of this, the spread of Misinformation and Disinformation is literally like wildfire, especially with the use of the social media platforms. In this book, we cover this topic in great detail by focusing on the following:

- What Misinformation and Disinformation are all about
- The role of Generative AI in Misinformation and Disinformation
- The role of social engineering in Misinformation and Disinformation
- The role of cyberbullying in Misinformation and Disinformation
- Tools to mitigate Misinformation and Disinformation

This will for sure be an explosive topic in the coming years for cybersecurity.

# Cyberterrorism
## The Rise of Misinformation and Disinformation

Ravi Das

CRC Press
Taylor & Francis Group
Boca Raton London New York

CRC Press is an imprint of the
Taylor & Francis Group, an **informa** business

Designed cover image: Shutterstock Image ID 2482142297

First edition published 2026
by CRC Press
2385 NW Executive Center Drive, Suite 320, Boca Raton FL 33431

and by CRC Press
4 Park Square, Milton Park, Abingdon, Oxon, OX14 4RN

*CRC Press is an imprint of Taylor & Francis Group, LLC*



ISBN: 978-1-041-07737-4 (hbk)
ISBN: 978-1-041-07831-9 (pbk)
ISBN: 978-1-003-64237-4 (ebk)

DOI: 10.1201/9781003642374

Typeset in Sabon
by SPi Technologies India Pvt Ltd (Straive)

This book is dedicated to my Lord and Savior, Jesus Christ, the Grand Designer of the Universe, and to my parents, Dr. Gopal Das and Mrs. Kunda Das.
And to my loving cats, Fifi and Bubu, and guinea pig, Noodles.
This book is also dedicated to:
Richard and Gwynda Bowman
Jaya Chandra
Tim Auckley
Patricia Bornhofen
Ashish Das
Caylee Gibbons
Rory Maxfield
Caylee Gibbons
Lynette Lambing

# Contents

# Acknowledgment

I would like to thank Ms. Gabriella Williams, my editor, who made this book a reality.

# Author biography

**Ravi Das** is a technical writer in the cybersecurity realm. He also does cybersecurity consulting on the side through his private practice, M L Tech, Inc. He also holds the Certified in Cybersecurity certification from the ISC(2).

Chapter 1

# An introduction to Misinformation and Disinformation

There was a time in the world when we could trust at face value the information and data that we received, whether it would be in our professional lives, personal lives, or just day-to-day watching of keeping up with the news headlines through whichever medium it may have come from. But, this was an age of innocence, and where all humans had the deep instinct that no level of harm would come in this regard. But, as technology has evolved over time, the ability to actually trust the information and data that we are receiving on a daily basis has declined greatly.

In fact, this has been most pronounced ever since 2020, when ChatGPT was launched by Open AI. With this, false and misleading information and data can be produced in just a matter of minutes, by merely submitting a few queries into the system. From here, once the output has been generated, it can be posted on all of the major social media platforms (most notably those of X, Facebook, Instagram, Pinterest, LinkedIn, etc.) in just a matter of seconds.

But, it is very important to keep in mind that is not just social media where misleading information and data can be posted. Even the most reputed of news sources can also fall prey to it as well, as share that with their respective audiences. Probably the biggest catalysts of this all are the political seasons, especially the presidential elections that take place here in the United States. One of the most widely used vehicles for this is known as "Deepfakes".

Essentially, these are replicated images and videos of real people that are spread mostly on social media sites. A perfect example of this would be a nominee from either one of the major parties (Democrat or Republican). In this case, a Cyberattacker could use the models and algorithms of Generative AI to create an impostor of that particular nominee. However, it would be nearly impossible to tell that it is actually fake until one were to take a very close look at it.

From here, the Cyberattacker can then post a Deepfake video on YouTube, asking for financial donations to be made to his or her campaign. But of course, any money sent would be simply sent to an offshore account,

DOI: 10.1201/9781003642374-1

making it almost impossible to recover in the end. Deepfakes and Generative AI will be covered in more detail in Chapter 2. It is very important to keep in mind that very distinct terms have now emerged for the misleading information and data. They are known technically as "Misinformation" and "Disinformation". They will be reviewed in the next section.

## MISINFORMATION AND DISINFORMATION

These two terms are used in conjunction with one another quite often, but they do have their key differences, which will be examined. But first, it is important to provide a technical definition of both of these terms. First, Misinformation can be defined as follows:

> Misinformation occurs when someone inadvertently spreads false information. Unlike disinformation, people who share misinformation do not intend to lie or deceive. Misinformation is simply false or inaccurate information — nothing more, nothing less.
>
> *Source: https://www.thefire.org/research-learn/misinformation-versus-disinformation-explained*

Now, Disinformation can be defined as follows:

> Disinformation, however, is false or misleading information peddled deliberately to deceive, often in pursuit of an objective.
>
> *Source: https://www.thefire.org/research-learn/misinformation-versus-disinformation-explained*

So as one can see from the above definitions, the key difference between the two is that the former is just simply spreading false information and news without actually double-checking the facts that go along with it. There are literally millions of examples of this, but probably one of the best ones at least that I (the author) can remember the best is the 2000 presidential election between Albert Gore and George W. Bush. There were a countless number of times when the major news outlets claimed that George W. Bush won the electoral votes of the state of Florida, but then recalled it, because the number of votes between him and Alber Gore were literally razor thin.

This is an example of Misinformation, where news was given, but the facts could not be checked in enough time. No harm or damage was ever intended.

But with the latter, ***there is a clear and distinct intention to do harm*** by spreading false information and data. Our previous example of Deepfakes clearly illustrates this. But to drive the point further, and to make it relevant to Cybersecurity, take the example of a Social Engineering Attack. In this regard, the primary intention of the Cyberattacker is to give false information and data about themselves in order to build up a trusting relationship over time with the victim.

Then once the timing is right, the Cyberattacker will then prey upon the vulnerable feelings of the victim in order to gain access to sensitive and confidential data, such as getting login credentials to the IT and Network Infrastructure of the business where the victim works at.

But, Misinformation and Disinformation are just the two general categories of misleading information and data. They both have subcategories, which are examined in the next section.

## THE SUBCATEGORIES OF MISINFORMATION AND DISINFORMATION

### Disinformation

First, the categories of Disinformation are as follows:

1. The Parody and/or Satire:
   This can be considered as poking fun or humor, in a perverse sense, toward the victim. Although no intentional harm has been originally intended, the victim still may feel a negative impact by it, when they view this as either a Bullying or a Cyberbullying attempt.
2. The False Connection:
   This is where the victim is purposely directly into making a negative connotation between two pieces of content. A good example of this is a news headline, as it relates to Cybersecurity. For example, it could read as follows:
   "Ransomware Attacks are Greatly Falling!!!"
   So while the headline portrays positive news, the image provided just below it portrays an entirely different meaning, which can cause a great amount of confusion, because it is the complete opposite. Images are also considered to be content, but of course, are graphical in nature.
3. The Misleading Content:
   In this particular case, it is about selectively any kind or type of content in order to support one's argument. While this is definitely a logical step to take, the harm comes when false information and data are used in order to support the argument. For example, if one were to make this statement: "Ransomware Attacks have decreased by at least 60%". But when quoting a number like this, it is very important to give the actual source of the data. Without it, one can safely assume that this specific number was simply, in order to support the observed statement.

4. The False Context:
   This is a case where the information and data presented is actually legitimate and authentic but is purposely being used in the wrong context in order to be deceiving. For example, suppose there is an actual fact stating that Endpoint Detection Response and Extended Detection Response can reduce the chances of a threat variant entering a device by at least 70%. Then, a competitor of the vendor who made this statement takes that fact and falsely claims that it is not a suitable solution for smartphones (which are technically considered endpoints). This is an instance where real data is used in the wrong context in an effort to overthrow that particular vendor.
5. The Impostor Content:
   This is the particular situation where the information and data that is presented is actually authentic and legitimate, but it is being conveyed by a person or an entity that is not genuine. The perfect example of this is the Deepfake, as it was pointed out earlier in this chapter. While what is being conveyed is real, the person delivering that message is not, as it is a replicated and spoofed-up version of a real human being. A good example of this is when the Cyberattacker creates a Deepfake video of an actual CEO and delivers a message from that in order to both deceive and con employees of that company.
6. The Manipulated Content:
   This is the situation where legitimate and authentic information is presented, but in a way that is designed to deceive the victim into giving out their own confidential information and data. The perfect example of this is that of Social Engineering. In this particular instance, the Cyberattacker is actually imitating somebody else with their real information and data, but is actually manipulating it in such a way that it is used to develop a trusting relationship with the victim, and as mentioned, preying upon their emotional state of mind. Then once the moment is right, the Cyberattacker will then prey upon this vulnerability, and convince them to do whatever is asked of them. In a way, it is a very basic form of brainwashing.
7. The Fabricated Content:
   This has been deemed to be ultimately one of the worst forms of Disinformation. For example, all of the information and data that is presented is completely false and is intended intentionally to cause grave harm to the victim. As it relates to Cybersecurity, a perfect example is that of a Phishing Email. The information and data that is presented from within the body of the message is completely false and is totally designed to lure the victim into committing an act that could cause harm to themselves. This can be in the form of downloading a malicious attachment or being redirected to a phony website, where the victim is lured into giving up their login credentials. An example of a victim receiving a Phishing email in this method is illustrated in Figures 1.1 and 1.2.

*Figure 1.1* This is an example of a false connection in disinformation.

**Source: https://www.shutterstock.com/image-photo/dark-hacker-computer-malware-screen-cybersecurity-2491655697**

*Figure 1.2* This is an example of a phishing email.

**Source: https://www.shutterstock.com/image-photo/business-woman-thinking-phone-spam-email-2264233913**

## Malinformation

There is yet another category (not a subcategory per se) of Disinformation, and this is known as specifically as "Malinformation". It can be technically defined as follows:

> It is the deliberate publication of private information for personal, corporate or political, rather than public interest, such as: revenge porn or leaking certain emails hacked in order to damage someone's reputation. It can also include deliberate change of context, date or time of the original content.
>
> *Source: https://commonslibrary.org/disinformation-and-7-common-forms-of-information-disorder/?gad_source=1&gclid=EAIaIQobChMI7cz0-ZzbiwMVzkf_AR0lsxxzEAMYASAAEgK-T_D_BwE#Download_Infographic*

A perfect example of this is the recent variants of Ransomware Attacks. If the Cyberattacker is successful in gaining any form of data, they can use that in an Extortion Attack in order to con the victim into paying up a set amount of money in order to prevent that data from being made available to the public.

## Misinformation

As it was earlier defined earlier in this chapter, Misinformation is the spreading of false information and data, but with no intent or desire to harm anybody. In a way, it can be viewed as merely hearing a rumor and repeating it to a person or a group of people. But whatever the case or situation might be, just like Disinformation, Misinformation also has its distinct set of subcategories, with the major ones being the following:

1. The Sockpuppet:
   These are also referred to as "Burner Accounts". Essentially, these are accounts that are created under false pretenses by real people. Its main purpose is to create drama or conflict between two (or more) parties. For example, this could be deliberately creating two fake events, both of which are aimed at supporters of opposing political parties, which are to be held at the same place, time, and day.
2. The Rumor:
   This is information and data that is shared without verification or confirming the evidence or the source of it. Good examples of these are those events that occur shortly after an incident (e.g., natural disaster or terrorist attack) when little information is known with certainty.
3. The Click Bait:
   These are merely sensationalized headlines that are specifically aimed in terms of attracting attention for readership. A perfect example of

this is the "Pay Per Click", also referred to commonly as just "PPC". In these cases, each time any kind or type of content is read online, the author owner of the advertisement receives a payment.

4. The Bot:
   A Bot can be technically defined as follows:

> A bot is an automated software application that performs repetitive tasks over a network. It follows specific instructions to imitate human behavior but is faster and more accurate. A bot can also run independently without human intervention. For example, bots can interact with websites, chat with site visitors, or scan through content. While most bots are useful, outside parties design some bots with malicious intent. Organizations secure their systems from malicious bots and use helpful bots for increased operational efficiency.
>
> *Source: https://aws.amazon.com/what-is/bot/*

The Bot is one of those subcategories that could also fit in with Disinformation as well. But as you can see from the above definition, Bots have served mostly a "good" purpose, which is used primarily for the purposes of automation. For example, Google makes use of Bots to scour the millions upon millions of websites that are available on the Internet. This is done in an effort to find the keywords in all of those websites in an effort to rank them appropriately in the Google Search Engines as end users conduct their searches on this platform. Another prime example of where Bots are used for good purposes is with Amazon. These are used constantly, on a 27 × 7 × 365 basis in order to analyze the thousands of pieces of content which is submitted to the Kindle Direct Publishing platform for self-publication. But on the flip side, the most malicious bots are those that are designed to influence opinions, especially in the political world, and around election seasons. These bots are generated and run by Automated Technology Systems (sometimes referred to as click farms or bot warehouses) and contribute to online discussions on a global basis.

## THE HISTORY OF MISINFORMATION AND DISINFORMATION

It should be noted that the spread of Misinformation and Disinformation is something that is very difficult to quantify. It is very qualitative in nature from the standpoint of scientific research. Thus, trying to figure out exactly when all of this started. One could surmise it first started with the birth of the first human beings on this planet, after all, they have to communicate with each other in some way, shape, or form. Perhaps this all started out as

Disinformation, with no intention of harm actually being done to the recipient who is actually receiving the information and data.

In this section of the chapter, we make great efforts to ascertain when the first cases of both Misinformation and Disinformation came about, and how it has proliferated since then.

## The Roman Empire

Roughly around 2000 years ago today, the Republic of Rome was in the beginnings of a massive civil war with Octavian (who was actually the adopted son of Julius Caesar), and Mark Anthony, who also happened to be one of Caesar's top military generals. But as we see in today's political environment, Octavian knew he had to have the public trust as well as sympathy on his side for the long term, in order to be a successful ruler.

In order to make this specifically happen, Octavian launched the proverbial "Fake News" campaign against his foe, Mark Anthony. This was done by making false claims he was having an affair with Cleopatra, the current Queen of Egypt. Apparently, she had no respect for the traditional Roman values and customs, such as faithfulness and respect. Octavian also falsified claims that Mark Anthony was unfit to hold office because of his massive drinking problem.

In order to get these kinds and types of falsehoods out the door, Octavian made heavy usage of both poetry and short, snappy slogans which were literally embedded into their main form of currency, which was the basic coin. But this all paid off, as Octavian eventually won the war, and ruled Rome for well for over 40 years.

## The 18th century

During this specific timeframe, many advancements were made in terms of the printing press technology. The prime example of this was the creation of the printing press known as the "Gutenberg". This happened in the late 15th century. As a result of these developments, this allowed for fake news to catalyze and spread faster than ever imagined before. This also led to the rapid creation of books and other printed materials that could be produced very quickly as opposed to just using the conventional means of handwriting.

Because of all of this, by the late 1700s, this led to the massive spread of fake news about King George II, of Great Britain and also Ireland. At the time, there was an uprising against the King, and thus, he needed the tools to make sure that the rebellion did not succeed by enhancing his image as a strong leader.

But before he could rebuild his image in the eyes of his own people, fake news about the King being in rapidly declining health was printed from sources from his opposition. Because of the rapid developments in the printing press, all of the false stories were being republished like wildfire. As a result of this, the King's public image further deteriorated, despite the fact that the rebellion was not successful in the end this perfectly exemplifies just fake news can be used to sway people's opinions rapidly.

The above-mentioned scenario actually has been credited for the fake stories that you see being published on social media sites on a daily basis. But, since hardly any human intervention is involved now because of the proliferation of Generative AI, there is hardly any fact-checking that is taking place. As a result of this, this kind of false information and data starts to be taken seriously and the more and quicker that it is shared.

## Life on the moon

We all know for a fact that the first humans to step onto the Moon happened back in July of 1969. In fact, for all we know, the people that made this trip were the first forms of life there as well. But, long before this event of the century actually happened, false news about the existence of life on the Moon already had started to precipitate. For example, by the late 19th century, the printing of newspapers became very cheap, and in some cases, one could even purchase a major newspaper for just a penny.

The perfect example of this was the New York Sun, in which a series of articles about possible life on the moon were printed in 1835 about life on the Moon. The life forms that were portrayed were rather exotic in both form and nature, such as unicorns, and two-flying human beings. These falsehoods were further solidified by the belief that a well-known astronomer had proof of the existence of this kind of life, and as a result of this, it helped people to believe this false story was actually true.

These false stories in the end became very popular, and as a result of this, the total sales of the paper drastically shot up, because of the curiosity that it left in the minds of the subscribers. This was despite the fact even the author of the articles knew the story was not at all true and had meant for this to be humorous and entertaining. This actually led to the birth of what is known as a "Satire". It can be technically defined as follows:

> Satire is the use of humor, irony, sarcasm, or ridicule to criticize something or someone. Public figures, such as politicians, are often the subject of satire, but satirists can take aim at other targets as well—from societal conventions to government policies. Satire is an entertaining form of social commentary, and it occurs in many forms: there are satirical novels, poems, and essays, as well as satirical films, shows, and cartoons.
>
> *Source: https://www.litcharts.com/literary-devices-and-terms/satire*

This is probably one of the most prominent forms of content on all of the major social media platforms of today. This is yet another form of fake news, and in fact, crosses even into the territory of being Disinformation.

### The rise of propaganda

This can also be considered as yet another form of Misinformation. In this regard, Propaganda can be technically defined as follows:

> Propaganda is the dissemination of information—facts, arguments, rumours, half-truths, or lies—to influence public opinion. It is often conveyed through mass media.
>
> *Source: https://www.britannica.com/topic/propaganda*

While in a theoretical sense, it is not designed to cause harm, it can if the victim takes the information and data the wrong way and uses it to do something that they would not normally do. One of the best examples of this is during the times of a pandemic. All the way back in 1918, the Influenza Pandemic killed an estimated 20–40 million people on a global basis. It became known as the "Spanish Flu", despite the fact that it originated at an army base in Kansas. It spread like wildfire during World War I. But, the rumors started to flurry about it being called the "Spanish Flu" because Spain remained a neutral country during this timeframe.

But, the nations fighting in the war did not want their respective populations to hear about the flu outbreak, so efforts could be devoted to winning the war. So to do this, the governments of these nations claimed that the virus was under control and even refused to publish any kind or type of health bulletin. The victims here were the population of Philadelphia of these Disinformation campaigns. So much so, that even the editors at a major newspaper refused to run news bulletins warning people about just how easily spread the flu was. Because of all of this, more than 12,000 Philadelphians died from the flu infection.

Finally, for a more detailed timeline of the history of Misinformation and Disinformation, access the link below:

> https://cyberresources.solutions/Cyberterrorism%20Book/Detailed_History.pdf

## REAL-WORLD EXAMPLES OF MISINFORMATION AND DISINFORMATION

There are plenty of real-world examples of Misinformation and Disinformation, and it is especially prevalent in today's political climate at least here in the United States. At this point in this chapter, there is no need to cover each and every one of them. But to highlight the ramifications of them, we have selected four cases, which are worthy of making note of. They are as follows:

1. The Use of WhatsApp Leads to Murder:

This was covered by the New York Times and made further use of both articles that combined both text and video to inform readers about what exactly transpired of the fake messages that were sent via WhatsApp that led to the deaths of 24 people.

More information about this can be accessed at the link below:

https://www.nytimes.com/interactive/2018/07/18/technology/whatsapp-india-killings.html?smid=pl-share

2. A Person Walks Into Washington, DC with an Assault Rifle:
   The Washington Post covered an incident in 2016 where a man entered a pizza restaurant in Washington DC and fired his weapon due to his belief that some fake news about himself originated from that location.

   More information about this can be accessed at the link below:

   https://www.washingtonpost.com/news/local/wp/2016/12/04/d-c-police-respond-to-report-of-a-man-with-a-gun-at-comet-ping-pong-restaurant/
3. Cover Ups:
   This was a story that was published by the New York Times. It describes how the Government of China heavily used Misinformation in order to cover up any truths about human rights violations that occurred in the province of Xinjiang.

   More information about this can be accessed at the link below:

   https://www.nytimes.com/interactive/2021/06/22/technology/xinjiang-uyghurs-china-propaganda.html?campaign_id=9&emc=edit_nn_20210623&instance_id=33644&nl=the-morning&regi_id=152543582&segment_id=61457&te=1&user_id=78133e40512c42bbd63f9cf99ff18f6f
4. Conspiracy Theories:
   This was a story that was also published by the New York Times. It covered how the National Butterfly Center was targeted by conspiracy theorists for cases of human smuggling. The end result of all of these falsehoods was that the center had to physically close down for the safety and protection of its employees.

   More information about this can be accessed at the link below:

   https://www.nytimes.com/2022/02/06/us/butterfly-center-texas.html?campaign_id=9&emc=edit_nn_20220207&instance_id=52392&nl=the-morning&regi_id=152543582&segment_id=81890&te=1&user_id=78133e40512c42bbd63f9cf99ff18f6f

## THE EFFECTS OF MISINFORMATION AND DISINFORMATION

The effects of both Misinformation and Disinformation can have detrimental effects on the victim who is the recipient of the false information and data. But there are a lot of variables that can impact the level of what is experienced. For example, some victims can just shrug it off like nothing has ever happened, and then there are those that are very vulnerable to it and can even go to extremes. In a way, this can be easily compared to Cyberbullying, which will be covered in a chapter later in this book.

It is important to keep in mind that the spread of Misinformation and Disinformation can happen at any place, at any time, and can be sent by any entity. But as it has been mentioned throughout this chapter, it is the political election cycles that this most happens.

But there are three broad categories of the effects, which are as follows:

1. The Fear of Uncertainty:
   This is where Disinformation and Misinformation thrive in the most. For example, once false information and data are spread virally, Individuals become extremely cautious and question the authenticity of it all. To counter this, many psychologists recommend use the of critical thinking, rigorous citing for the actual facts, and accessing accurate record-keeping files.
2. The Depths of Polarization:
   Both Misinformation and Disinformation can trigger huge societal divisions and polarization. As communities and populations become more divided, there is a risk that individuals will become very selective in their acceptance of information and data based on their pre-existing beliefs, no matter what the real facts say. One of the best ways that this can be countered is through the use and implementation of thorough and complete documentation in order to present and provide an objective and unbiased view of what is really transpiring, thus promoting transparency and trust. The best example of this is what is happening today here in the United States. For instance, the current presidential administration has set up a shell of the Federal Government, called the "Department Of Government Efficiency", also known as "DOGE". Its so-called leader has not even been confirmed by the United States Senate, nor has this particular individual even been elected by the American People to be in this kind of role. Further, "DOGE" is not even an official department per se of the United States Federal Government. But despite all of this, baseless claims are constantly being made that mass layoffs have to happen in order to reduce the gargantuan size of the United States Deficit. However, no scientific evidence has been provided for this. But the core political base, which is known as "Make America Great Again", or "MAGA", through their pre-existing beliefs have not, nor will they ever question the rationality, legality, or the logic behind what is happening.
3. The Emotions:
   The virality nature of Disinformation and Misinformation often exploits the gamut of negative emotions, such as fear, anger, and absolutely no level of trust, in an effort to completely manipulate the victim into believing false or misleading information. Also, as it was just

stated, extremely detailed documentation must provide a source of reliable, evidence-based information, in order to further mitigate the impact of emotional manipulation. Also, the spread of Misinformation and Disinformation has an undeniable, macro impact on free speech, as we are seeing now here in the United States. In fact, as it relates to Cybersecurity, this is also exactly how Social Engineering is carried out. It can be technically defined as follows:

> Social engineering is a manipulation technique that exploits human error to gain private information, access, or valuables. In cybercrime, these "human hacking" scams tend to lure unsuspecting users into exposing data, spreading malware infections, or giving access to restricted systems. Attacks can happen online, in-person, and via other interactions.
>
> *Source: https://www.kaspersky.com/resource-center/definitions/what-is-social-engineering*

In other words, when a Cyberattacker engages in a Social Engineering Attack, they are literally trying to prey upon the vulnerable emotions and state of the mind of their victim in order to build up a trusting relationship. Once this has been established, they will then move into the proverbial "kill". An example of the different variants of Social Engineering can be seen in Figure 1.3.

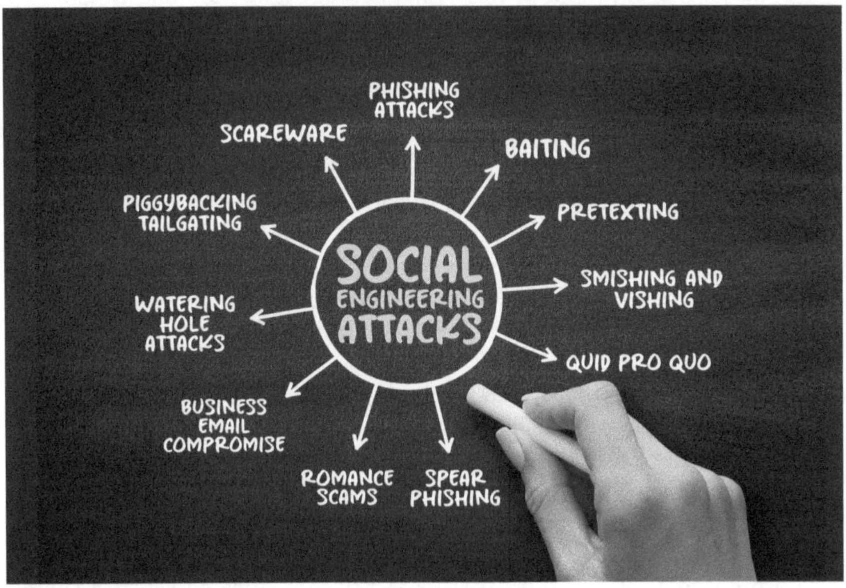


*Figure 1.3* This is an example of social engineering.

**Source: https://www.shutterstock.com/image-photo/social-engineering-attacks-psychological-manipulation-people-2339650091**

## The intents of Misinformation and Disinformation

The malicious "Intents" of Misinformation and Disinformation can fall into three distinct categories, which are as follows:

1. The Deceptive Intent:
   This set can be technically defined as follows:

   > It is purposefully designed to mislead, typically with motives rooted in political, ideological, or economic interests, amplifying its inherent threat.
   >
   > *Source: https://huridocs.org/2023/12/the-harmful-effects-of-disinformation-and-how-to-combat-them/*

   As an example of this, this is exactly where Social Engineering perfectly fits in, as just reviewed in the last subsection of this chapter.
2. The Coordinated Campaign:
   This set can be technically defined as follows:

   > It is orchestrated by both state and non-state actors, exploit weaknesses in the information ecosystem to propagate disinformation on a larger scale.
   >
   > *Source: https://huridocs.org/2023/12/the-harmful-effects-of-disinformation-and-how-to-combat-them/*

   The perfect example of this is happening right now and here in the United States, with the mass layoffs that are happening with the employees of the different branches of the United States Federal Government, carried by DOGE, as reviewed earlier in this chapter.
3. The Undermining of Trust:
   This set can be technically defined as follows:

   > The Disinformation and Misinformation acts as a corrosive force, eroding faith in institutions, fostering division within communities, and challenging the fundamental principles of human rights.
   >
   > *Source: https://huridocs.org/2023/12/the-harmful-effects-of-disinformation-and-how-to-combat-them/*

   Once again, the perfect example of this is the political climate that the population of the United States is currently facing. As it was once again reviewed, the leader of DOGE is making complete falsehoods in terms of the statistics as to why all of the mass firings are needed. This takes concrete statistical proof, which at the time of the writing of this book, has not even been presented yet. This in the end will simply erode the trust and faith that we Americans once had in our United States Federal Government.

## Ways to mitigate the intents of Misinformation and Disinformation

There are a number of key ways that one or any entity can take to help mitigate the above mentioned Intents to not only spread, but to not even become a victim of Misinformation and Disinformation. They are as follows:

1. The Verification:
   You need to make sure that the information and data that is collected is well-documented, sourced, and traceable to reliable origins. In this regard, the cross-referencing of the received data and information between various sources helps in verifying the accuracy of it all. When discrepancies arise, they can be investigated and resolved.
2. The Integrity:
   In this regard, you need to maintain a very rigorous and consistent process for data collection and storage. This is needed to preserve the integrity of information used in all sorts of content, which include reports, publications, and campaigns.
3. The Accuracy:
   Your business should maintain meticulous and detailed records of all types and kinds of activities, data, and findings. This documentation ensures the accuracy and validity of the information and data that has been disseminated to the public at large. The primary purpose for all of this is that you will need this documentation in order to counter-argue any pieces of Misinformation and Disinformation that have been spread about your business.
4. The Advocacy:
   You also need to have well-documented evidence to counter any claims of Misinformation and Disinformation that have been leveraged against your business.
5. The Transparency:
   You need to have both documentation and specific methodologies that will clearly demonstrate the level of transparency to foster trust with key stakeholders and the public at large. All of this will allow for open access to independent scrutiny and verification of the information and data that your business has.
6. The Context:
   You also need to have an extremely accurate document that reflects the context in which the information and data are presented. This will allow for any claims of Misinformation and Disinformation that are leveraged against your business to be negated.
7. The Level of Preparedness:
   You should also develop robust and effective crisis management protocols. This will help to ensure that a very quick and effective response

can be launched when your business is charged with Misinformation and Disinformation campaigns.

8. The Use of Technology:
   It is very important for you to harness the use of advanced technologies, such as Generative AI. It is very powerful so that you will have the ability to monitor the propagation of Misinformation and Disinformation and to detect malicious activities that pose a grave threat to your employees, customers, and key stakeholders that are involved with your business.

## HOW MISINFORMATION AND DISINFORMATION ARE EVOLVING INTO CYBERSECURITY

As it has been reviewed throughout this chapter, the use of both Misinformation and Disinformation can happen at any point in time, and any entity or any victim can feel the brunt of it, to varying degrees. As it was also noted, one of the times that the most damage occurs as a result of the spread of Misinformation and Disinformation is during the election cycles here in the United States, especially during the Presidential Elections, as we have seen since 2016.

But, there is yet another area in which Misinformation and Disinformation can have a huge impact, and that is in the realm of Cybersecurity. Many people and entities very often fail to realize when this actually happens, because the lines can become so easily blurred. For example, many people are aware of the effects of Phishing and Ransomware. With the former, most people know not to open up an email that is sent from somebody they do not know, or worse yet, open up a suspicious attachment or a link that is embedded into the body of the email. With the latter, probably not as many people have been impacted by it, but given all of the news headlines, people have at least heard about it.

But to a person who works in Cybersecurity, you will know that the impact has happened when it impacts a digital asset. This can be technically defined as follows:

> Digital assets refer to any piece of information or data stored electronically that holds value to an organization, including things like customer data, financial records, intellectual property, sensitive documents, website content, software applications, and even digital representations of physical assets.
>
> *Source: https://www.google.com/search?q=what+are+digital+assets+in+cyber+security&sca_esv=74940b13bb8c626e&source=hp&ei=dUDGZ_bTCJXbptQP4p6dqAE&iflsig=ACkRmUkAAAAAZ8ZOhUzaX9dZANnHh9GxGPOLn5-K9OLG&oq=what+is+a+digital+asset+in+cyber&gs_lp=Egdnd3Mtd2l6IiB3aGF0IGlzIGEgZGlnaXRhbCBhc3*

*NldCBpbiBjeWJlcioCCAAyBhAAGBYYHjILEAAY
gAQYhgMYigUyCxAAGIAEGIYDGIoFMgs
QABiABBiGAxiKBTIIEAAYgAQYogQyBRAAGO
8FMggQABiABBiiBDIIEAAYogQYiQUyCBAAGIAEGKIESJ
pWUABY4jhwB3gAkAEBmAGvAaAB4haqAQQzMy42
uAEByAEA-AEBmAItoALGFsICCxAAGIAEGLED
GIMBwgIOEC4YgAQYsQMY0QMYxwHCAgUQABiAB
MICCxAuGIAEGLEDGIMBwgIOEAAYgAQYsQMYgwEYi
gXCAg4QLhiABBixAxiDARjUAsICEBAAGIAEGLEDG
IMBGIoFGArCAgcQABiABBgKwgITEC4YgAQYsQMY0QMYgw
EYxwEYCsICChAAGIAEGLEDGArCAg0QABiABBix
AxiDARgKwgIREC4YgAQYsQMY0QMYgwEYx
wHCAggQABiABBixA5gDAJIHBDQwLjWgB8uRAg&
sclient=gws-wiz*

A more technical name for these pieces of information and data is known as "Personal Identifiable Information" datasets, or also known simply as "PII" for short. Although this was not included in the above definition, a digital asset can also be a vehicle that actually stores the PII datasets. Probably one of the best examples of this is the database that houses them. Although this can still be found in an On-Premises Infrastructure, most of these databases are now created into a major Cloud-based platform, such as that of the AWS or Microsoft Azure.

## The characteristics of a digital asset

Digital assets possess the following characteristics:

1. It Is Intangible:
   Unlike physical assets, digital assets are intangible and can be easily replicated and accessed by multiple users, if the proper rights, permissions, and privileges have not been assigned.
2. Its Degree of Vulnerability:
   Due to their unphysical nature, digital assets are susceptible to various cyber threats like data breaches, Ransomware attacks, phishing scams, and unauthorized access.
3. Its Need for Controls:
   Proper and effective security controls are crucial to safeguard digital assets, including encryption, access controls, data backups, and regular vulnerability assessments.

## The different types of digital assets

It is also important to note that there are different types of digital assets, which are as follows:

1. The Data Types:
   This can include such items as financial records, employee data, medical records, trade secrets, and source code.
2. The System Assets:
   These include such items as operating systems, servers, network devices, applications, and databases. Typically, you will find these in a Cloud-based deployment.
3. The Digital Currency:
   These are Cryptocurrencies like Bitcoin, Ethereum, and other blockchain-based tokens.
4. The Content Assets:
   These include such items as images, videos, audio files, documents.
5. The Access Credentials:
   These are the digital assets that are used to confirm the identity of an and grant access to share resources, they include: usernames, passwords, API keys, and digital certificates. A very important area here is the Privileged Access Management (PAM) credentials as well, as they are deemed to be "superuser in nature".

## How to manage a digital asset

There are numerous ways in which a Digital Asset should be managed, and they include the following:

1. The Asset Classification:
   This is the categorization of digital assets based on sensitivity and business impact (such as high, medium, and low) in an effort to prioritize protection.
2. The Access Control:
   This is the implementation of strong authentication methods and user permission levels to limit unauthorized access to the digital assets.
3. The Data Encryption:
   This is the process of encrypting sensitive data at rest and in transit to prevent unauthorized access even if breached.
4. The Continuous Monitoring:
   This is the regular scanning for suspicious activity and potential vulnerabilities across the digital landscape.

## The overall risks of Misinformation and Disinformation to cybersecurity

There are a number of key intersection points where the rise of Misinformation and Disinformation actually does intersect with the world of Cybersecurity in every aspect. In this subsection of this chapter, we take a look at key, six areas. They are as follows:

1. It Is Cheap:
   When compared to the other Cyber based Threat Variants, such as Ransomware, both Misinformation and Disinformation are actually a very inexpensive way to launch an attack on a business. This has given birth to what is known as "Disinformation as a Service", or "DaaS". This kind of service is available on the Dark Web, and to show just how affordable it is to spread online misinformation, DaaS providers charge as little as $15.00–$45.00 per 1,000-character piece of written content, plus an additional $65 to contact a media source that will spread the material. In sharp comparison, launching a Ransomware Attack costs, on average, $1,000 each and every time that it is done.
2. No Boundaries:
   One of the biggest risks of Misinformation and Disinformation is that it can originate from anywhere on the planet, at anytime, and impact kind or type of victim. According to this quote:

   > Bad actors — ranging from state-sponsored trolls to members of extremist groups to independent disinformation-service providers — can engage in all of these types of campaigns for reasons that range from greater notoriety to fee-for-service to ad revenue to secondary economic gain (e.g. product sales) to political and policy objectives.
   > *Source: The Future Of Disinformation Operations and The Coming War On Brands*

   Another main catalyst for the rapid and viral spread of Misinformation and Disinformation is purely the Internet. With all of its connectivity now, this means that online Misinformation and Disinformation can come from anyone around the world, thus impacting the victim literally thousands of miles away. This new kind of Threat Variant can from activists, extremists, conspiracy theorists, and trolls. In other words, it is not the nation state threat actors that are the main culprit now, as they have been for Ransomware Attacks. These primarily include the likes of China, Russia, Iran, and China.
3. The Quickness:
   Once a specific Misinformation and Disinformation Threat Variant has been launched it is extremely difficult to put a stop to it, because of its viral nature. In other words, once it is launched and deployed, the damage has already been done, in fact even quicker than a Ransomware Attack. In fact, a scientific study that was conducted by MIT in 2019 found that Misinformation and Disinformation spread farther, faster, and deeper than the real data, because of the Internet, and

all of the resources online that it is connected to. The results of their study found that news reports consisting of Misinformation and Disinformation are 70% more likely to be retweeted on the social media platform of "X", and even more shocking, it reaches the first 1,500 people six times faster.

The study also discovered that it can be difficult for a victim to segregate out identify true and false information and data. Even worse yet, it was found that it is real human beings that are the ones whom are spreading and amplifying the Misinformation and Disinformation.

4. The Legalities:
Another key catalyst why Misinformation and Disinformation pose such a grave risk to Cybersecurity is that believe it or not, it's completely legal to do. In other words, there is no formal law that has been enacted which regulates and controls the spread of false information and data. For example, Search Engines, such as Google and Bing and the major social media platforms of Linked In, Facebook, X, Instagram, Pinterest, etc. have no obligations whatsoever to configure their algorithms to reduce the risk of Misinformation and Disinformation.
This quote sums it up nicely:

> Other times, the only cause for redress is legal action, such as a defamation lawsuit, and those can be time-consuming and expensive to pursue.
>
> *Source: https://www.axios.com/2021/07/16/disinformation-business-security*

5. The Expense:
Just like a Ransomware Attack, or for that matter any type or kind of Cyberattack, launching Misinformation and Disinformation can cost the global economy at least $78 billion on an annualized basis. It can also cost the private sector on a global basis at least $100 billion on an annualized basis. In stark comparison, Deloitte estimates that a low-end Cyber Threat Variant could cost a business only about $25,000.00
6. The Relation to E-Commerce:
E-commerce has been around for the long time, making its first big splash back in the late 1990s, during the height of the Internet Bubble. But, as Misinformation and Disinformation came along, it put these online stores much more at a higher level of Cybersecurity Risk. This is easily done by deceiving their customers' shoppers in many different ways, even by redirecting them to a replicated, fake site of the real online merchant. A lot of this has now been fueled by Generative AI, especially when it comes to Deepfakes and phony Chatbots are made to look like the real thing. With the latter, the customer and/or prospect can be easily "suckered" into thinking that they are having a legitimate chat session, which is far from the truth. This is yet also another type and kind of Social Engineering, but this time it is happening in the digital world.

Also, E-commerce-based algorithms can also be used to trick the prospect and/or customer into recommending products that have darker meanings. As a result of this, brands that put their products and services onto an online store must be diligent about monitoring the online conversations that people are having about them, in order to identify and address Misinformation and Disinformation that is spread by the algorithms or even real people.

To view a more detailed report on the effects of Misinformation and Disinformation on an online merchant that is a small to medium sized business, click on the link below:

https://cyberresources.solutions/Cyberterrorism%20Book/Misinformation_Disinformation_Effects_On_Business.pdf

## HOW TO DISCERN IF YOU ARE A VICTIM OF A MISINFORMATION AND DISINFORMATION CYBERATTACK

As it has been reviewed at numerous places throughout this chapter, knowing when you have been exposed to any type or kind of Misinformation and Disinformation can be a very daunting task. The primary reason for this is that as human beings, we are completely connected to anything and everything in both the virtual and physical worlds.

We are exposed to so much of stimuli in the external environment that it is almost close to impossible to tell what is real or even fake anymore. If one were to put the blame on this, it could come from three distinct areas:

- The rapid advances that are being made in wireless technologies, not only entice us but even force us to make our smartphones a literal extension of our personal and professional lives. In other words, if we lose it or it gets stolen, a total feeling of paralysis will soon ensue.
- The rapid changes that are happening so quickly in Generative AI. This forces human beings even more to be connected into the external environment, from both the physical and virtual perspectives.
- The increasing addiction of human beings to the major social media platforms which include Linked In, Facebook, Instagram, X, Pinterest, etc.

But, there are some clues that you can look for in order to discern if you have been an actual recipient of Misinformation and Disinformation. Here they are:

1. The Response:
   When you receive a piece of information or data, does it make you invoke a specific kind of response? Sure, all of the stimuli in the external environment will provoke something out of you, but does this

one provoke an extreme one, that you normally do not feel? A perfect example of this is the traditional, Phishing email. This kind of stimulus normally strikes a fear or a strong sense of urgency to act on something very quickly. In other words, emotions that you normally do not feel on a daily basis. If you are feeling these kinds of sensations when you receive anything that is visual or written, you have most likely become the recipient of Misinformation and Disinformation.

2. The Kind of Statement:
   When you receive an actual piece of information and/or data, does it make a "bold" kind of statement that you normally do not see in the daily content that you come across? Or more specifically, is it addressing some kind or type of controversial issue? Some good examples of this at least here in the United States are those hot-button topics such as pro-life/prochoice, issues surrounding Diversity, Equity, and Inclusion (just recently now being known as simply "DEI"), any kind or type of religion, etc. Normally, when such pieces of content are generated and posted somewhere (usually on a major social media platform), sources and references are often cited for making these kinds of controversial claims. If none are present, then most likely you can be assured that you have become the recipient of Misinformation and Disinformation.
3. The Claims:
   Whenever you receive a piece of information or data, does it make claims that seem to be totally out of the ordinary? A good example of this is the pieces of content that are both written and visual, making claims to lose a drastic amount of weight in a short period of time, by taking either a supplement or some kind of drug. Normally, in these kinds of situations, once again, references and sources have to be cited to further substantiate any "out of the ordinary" claims that are being made. If none are present, then you can be more or less assured that you have become the recipient of Misinformation and Disinformation. When it comes to Cybersecurity, another good example of this is the vendors who boast that their products and/or solutions can cut down the instances that your employees fall for a Phishing Attack. While making such claims are actually needed in order to increase the believability of their products and/or solutions, they have to be once again, backed up by sources and references to substantiate these claims. If none are there, then there are good chances, that these are simply pieces of Misinformation and Disinformation.
4. The Clickbait:
   This can be technically defined as follows:

   > Something (such as a headline) designed to make readers want to
   > something (such as a headline) designed to make readers want to

*Figure 1.4* This is an example of Clickbait.

**Source: https://www.shutterstock.com/image-photo/clickbait-content-web-click-button-risk-2358680237**

> click on a hyperlink especially when the link leads to content of dubious value or interest on a hyperlink especially when the link leads to content of dubious value or interest.
>
> *Source: https://www.merriam-webster.com/dictionary/clickbait*

Another perfect example of this is once again, the Phishing email. If it does not contain a malicious attachment, then most likely contains a link that will entice you to click on it. But in the end, it will only take you to a phony website in which your login credentials will only be covertly heisted. An example of Clickbait can be seen in Figure 1.4.

5. The Small Pieces:

This kind of content consists of small bits of information and data that are actually legitimate and authentic, but when they are collectively overly exaggerated, you then know for sure that you have become the recipient of Misinformation and Disinformation. Also, the end result is an overall piece of content that has become grossly misleading and could cause potential harm to the victim at hand.

## HOW TO MITIGATE THE RISKS OF BECOMING A VICTIM OF MISINFORMATION AND DISINFORMATION

So far in this chapter, we have covered the concepts of both Misinformation and Disinformation from a number of different perspectives, which include the following:

- Misinformation and Disinformation.
- The Subcategories of Misinformation and Disinformation (Malinformation was reviewed).
- The History of Misinformation and Disinformation.
- Real World Examples of Misinformation and Disinformation.
- The Effects of Misinformation and Disinformation.
- How Misinformation and Disinformation Are Evolving Into Cybersecurity (an extensive of the impacts upon the Digital Assets was also provided).
- How to Discern if You Are a Victim of a Misinformation and Disinformation Cyberattack.

After covering all of this, the next question that you might be having is: "How do avoid From being a Victim Of Misinformation and Disinformation?" Well, in this regard, it is important to consider that any and all content that you come across, in both the physical and virtual worlds, can be considered as a potential Threat Variant from the standpoint of Cybersecurity. Thus in this regard, one truly cannot be a victim of a Threat Variant, such as that of Phishing and Ransomware. The secret key here is in learning how to lessen or mitigate the statistical chances, or odds, of happening to you. In this section of this book, we look at some ways that you can use it.

1. Be Double-Checking:
   In this regard, whatever your sources of information and data are, you have to try to double-check them as much as you can. Here are some key quotes to drive this point further:
   a. "If it's coming through your Twitter, Facebook or Instagram feed, don't think of it as information from those platforms, because it's not."
   b. "Ask yourself, 'Who is this coming from and what is the background?'"
   c. For example, the U.S. Department of State recently identified disinformation campaigns about the coronavirus in Europe, "Ruston said. In those cases, strident claims about dangers to residents were made in order to undermine the government." (Source: https://news.asu.edu/20200407-solutions-7-ways-protect-yourself-against-misinformation).

   Although checking out the viability of any information and data that you receive may seem like a time-consuming task, ***it is important you***

***don't have to check all of the time.*** If you do, it could literally become its own full-time. Rather, go back to that specific rule of thumb that was reviewed earlier in this chapter: Always trust your gut, and if you feel and emotional response come through that seems to be out of the ordinary, then check your sources. But also, keep this one perspective in mind as well: ***Never use Generative AI in of itself to check the validity of the information and data that you receive.*** The reason for this is pure and simple: There is no guarantee that the outputs that are generated are even valid, because you do not know if the datasets that have been fed into it are actually cleansed and optimized. Therefore, the best advice is then to manually check for yourself, using something very reliable like the Google Search Engine.

2. The Social Media:
One cardinal rule of thumb when it comes to receiving information and data at your disposal is to never trust any kind or type of social media platform in the first instance. For example, even with Facebook, your family member's or friend's account could have been covertly hacked into, and they can easily put in Misinformation and Disinformation that actually seems to be believable. Also, as it was examined earlier, even Deepfakes can be used to open an entirely phony account tricking you into believing that is somebody that you actually know. Consider these quotes to further drive home the above:
    a. "When someone asks you where you heard something, if your first inclination is to say Twitter, you need to stop and check because Twitter itself tells you nothing,"
    b. "Twitter gives people a feed of people who will tell you things," she said. "Ask questions like, 'What's the actual post?' 'What's the thing that's telling you this piece of information?' 'Who is that person?' 'Is it a media organization you've ever heard of before?'"
    c. "You can find all of that information in a Twitter profile. There's basic information you can find with a millisecond of extra effort. People who have credibility generally put information in their bios to bolster their credibility." (Source: https://news.asu.edu/20200407-solutions-7-ways-protect-yourself-against-misinformation).

    In fact, to make the above points relevant to Cybersecurity, view any information and data that you receive on a social media platform as a Phishing email. In other words, always view it suspiciously, and proceed with caution before clicking on anything. If you have further doubts about anything, always confirm the validity of the information and data with the person who posted. For example, if you were to receive a Phishing email, the cardinal rule is always to confirm with the sender of the email if they have actually sent the message or not. Remember, the Cyberattacker of today can easily heist your address book from your contact list on your smartphone. By having that in their possession, they can easily craft and send a Phishing based email that looks it was sent from somebody in your contact list.

3. The Sources:
   Probably ever since you have learned in your days in college, especially when you wrote term papers, one of the key things that your professor taught you is to always cite your sources, whether you are taking a direct quote, or including hardcore data, such as statistics. The same can also be said of any and all of the information and data that you receive. Make sure that all said claims are backed up and cited with genuine sources, and that they follow a recognized format for the actual citing. Consider these quotes to further understand the sheer importance of this:

   > "Look for how sources are treated and referenced."
   >
   > "Journalists that work for traditional news outlets like AZCentral, CNN and the New York Times have a set of professional ethics guidelines and will assert their sources. The best is when the sources are named, the next best is when the names have been concealed for the protection of the source."
   >
   > "However, it's appropriate to be skeptical of articles that depend solely on unattributed sources without any kind of corroboration."
   >
   > *Source: https://news.asu.edu/20200407-solutions-7-ways-protect-yourself-against-misinformation*

   In other words, if you come across any piece of information or data that you may receive, always check to see if any sources have been cited. If they do not look to be very legitimate or if they do not appear to be organized in any kind or type of coherent manner, then you are very likely the recipient of Misinformation and Disinformation.
4. The Level of Reading:
   At the very beginning of this chapter, an example of Disinformation was provided with regard to Ransomware Attacks. For example, the headline said that Ransomware Attacks were actually falling, but just underneath that, was an image of an actual Ransomware Attack that was taking place. The sheer moral of the story here is not to just simply make an informed opinion just based upon reading the headline only. Always read or see the content just below it to see just how well it supports the actual headline before you form your opinion. To understand the gravity of this, consider these quotes:
   a. "It's important to read the story fully,"
   b. "Very often, headlines are misleading and are not there to inform you."
   c. "The purpose of the headline is to get you to click on the link or to buy the newspaper, or to tune in if you're channel surfing."

   *Source: https://news.asu.edu/20200407-solutions-7-ways-protect-yourself-against-misinformation*
5. The Variety:
   In this regard, in order to further mitigate the risk of becoming a recipient of Misinformation and Disinformation, get your information

and data from a wide variety of sources, whatever they may be. But as it relates to Cybersecurity, if a news headline of a security breach comes out, it is very important first to give time for the story to evolve. The primary reason for this is that you really do not know if it is a fake headline or not. Also, collecting the facts takes time to evolve. Thus, your best bet would be to reach out to any of the following sources in order to confirm the facts:

a. A reputable IT Services Provider.
b. A reputable Managed Solutions Provider (also known as an "MSSP").
c. A reputable Managed Security Solutions Provider (also known as an "MSSP").
d. A reputable Cloud Services Provider (also known as a "CSP").

These above-mentioned entities should have access to the most up-to-date information and data about a security breach, but above all, this is what they do on a 24 × 7 × 365 basis, so you can be more or less guaranteed that the information and data you receive from them will be reasonably accurate. To make this point clearer, consider the following quote:

> "If you read something and if your reaction is any sort of extreme emotion, outrage or unmitigated joy, that's a clear indicator that you should definitely read more deeply."
>
> "Many of the disinformation examples we've come across in our research are designed not to inform but rather to activate a strong anger or fear response."
>
> *Source: https://news.asu.edu/20200407-solutions-7-ways-protect-yourself-against-misinformation*

6. Keep Sharing:

One of the most well-known ways that Misinformation and Disnformation can go virally is via gossip. Therefore, if you are in a gathering with your family and friends, and you hear information and data that appear to be not true, it is very important that you correct them by stating that they should confirm whatever information and data that they have received. To further ramify this point, consider the quote below:

> "Always be kind when helping people identify misinformation. Don't insult people's intelligence."
>
> "Don't repeat lies, because when you emphasize the thing that they got wrong, they're actually cognitively more likely to remember the thing they got wrong. You want to provide them with new information that comes from a source as reputable as possible."
>
> *Source: https://news.asu.edu/20200407-solutions-7-ways-protect-yourself-against-misinformation*

7. Check Others:
   Just like it was mentioned in point #6, apart from using other, varied sources for getting your information and data, you should also check out areas of information and data that are similar to what you are also the recipient of. If they all follow the same, parallel path and direction, then you can be more or less assured that the information and data that you have received are not Misinformation or Disinformation. But if they are far apart, then you have to do your own investigation, as it has been detailed throughout this entire chapter.

   To make this point clearer, consider the following quotes:

   a. "I really believe in expertise, which is why I really like NPR as a news source because there is deep expertise both from perspective of journalistic integrity and in selection of credible sources."
   b. "I've actually done this where somebody will tweet something and I would think, 'That's interesting, I wonder if it's true.' Then, I will go separately into a Google search and pull up the news articles on it and see what's written about that topic." (Source: https://news.asu.edu/20200407-solutions-7-ways-protect-yourself-against-misinformation)

## DISINFORMATION AS A SERVICE

As we wrap this chapter, we are going to provide a more extensive review of a concept that was reviewed earlier in this chapter: Disinformation As a Service, also known as "DaaS" for short. It can be technically defined as follows:

> Disinformation-as-a-Service (DaaS) is a new model of information warfare where anyone can buy fake news and misinformation campaigns and spread them across the internet. DaaS is made possible by a network of professional trolls, bots, and other online manipulation tools readily available for hire.
>
> *Source: https://hackernoon.com/disinformation-as-a-service-content-marketings-evil-twin*

Typically, to keep things as covert as possible, primarily to avoid the Federal Law Enforcement such as the United States Secret Service and the FBI, all the DaaS is usually available on the Dark Web. With this, the Cyberattacker can literally outsource a group of individuals to do all of this for literally pennies on the dollar. By making use of this kind of particular service, there are two primary driving factors:

- To achieve any amount of financial gain that is possible.

- Reputation Damage: This can be technically defined as follows:

> Reputational damage is the loss to financial capital, social capital and/or market share resulting from damage to an organization's reputation. This is often measured in lost revenue, increased operating, capital or regulatory costs, or destruction of shareholder value.
>
> *Source: https://en.wikipedia.org/wiki/Reputational_damage*

The kinds and types of resources that a Cyberattacker has at their disposal by using are as follows:

1. The Troll Farms:
   These professional operators generate fake news and other forms of online Misinformation. They are often located in the countries that are deemed to be nation-state threat actors, such as Russia, China, Iran, and North Korea.
2. The Bots:
   These are typically the automated accounts that spread vast amounts of Misinformation and Disinformation within minutes on a global basis. They can be used to create a fake sense of group consensus or to silence the opposing points of view.
3. The Fake News Sites:
   These are typically the websites that publish fabricated pieces of information and data that are designed specifically to deceive and mislead. The perfect example of this was during the COVID-19 pandemic. Cyberattackers would often resort to what is known as "Domain Squatting". This can be technically defined as follows:

> It is the practice of registering an internet domain name that is very similar to a well-known trademark or company name with the malicious intent to profit from it, typically by directing users to a different website.
>
> *Source: what is domain squatting - Google Search: https://www.google.com/search?q=what+is+domain+squatting&sca_esv=887cc09dfdb753d2&source=hp&ei=bp7LZ7jMN-XE0PEP0uGrmQ0&iflsig=ACkRmUkAAAAAZ8usfh0rgax2DHdT8DjAnlxS72RRnnIc&ved=0ahUKEwi4u__Rq_mLAxVlIjQIHdLwKtMQ4dUDCBA&uact=5&oq=what+is+domain+squatting&gs_lp=Egdnd3Mtd2l6GgIYAiIYd2hhdCBpcyBkb21haW4gc3F1YXR0aW5nMgUQABiABDIGEAAYFhgeMgYQABgWGB4yBhAAGBYYHjILEAAYgAQYhgMYigUyCxAAGIAEGIYDGIoFMgUQABjvBTIIEAAYgAQYogRI3DRQAFirMnABeACQAQGYAW-gAYMPqgEEMjMuMrgBA8gBAPgBAZgCGaAC_g7CAgoQABiABBhDGIoFwgILEAAYgAQYkQIYigXCAhAQABiABBixAxhDGIMBGIoFwgILEAAYgAQYsQMYgw*

*HCAg4QLhiABBixAxjRAxjHAcICFhAuGIAEGLEDGNE DGEMYgwEYxwEYigXCAg4QABiABBixAxiDARiKBcICCx AAGIAEGLEDGIsDwgIREAAYgAQYsQMYgw EYigUYiwPCAggQABiABBiLA8ICCBAAGIAEGLED wgIIEAAYFhgKGB6YAwDiAwUSATEgQJIHB DIzLjKgB6eaAQ&sclient=gws-wiz*

For example, we all know that Walmart, the retail giant, has a very strong brand name reputation, and its domain is the following:

https://www.walmart.com/

But, to create the fake website, a Cyberattacker can register a domain name that is eerily close to it, such as:

https://www.walmmart.com/

From here, the Cyberattacker will then create a fake website that looks like a legitimate Walmart site. It is important to note that most people don't pay careful attention to the syntax of the domain name that they are going into, thus, that is why they are so easy to fall prey for this kind of tactic by the Cyberattacker.

4. The Social Media:
   The major platforms of X (formerly Twitter), Facebook, Linked In, Instagram, Pinterest, etc. are deemed to be the major culprits of the virality spread of both Misinformation and Disinformation, because just about anything and everything imaginable can be put onto them, especially Deepfakes (which will be reviewed in the next chapter of this book).
5. The Influencers:
   This is where the Cyberattacker, through making use of the tactics and concept of Social Engineering can influence social media users with large followings to spread large amounts of Misinformation and Disinformation.

## HOW DISINFORMATION AS A SERVICE IS LAUNCHED

Although it is entirely up to the Cyberattacker how they plan to launch a Misinformation and Disinformation Threat Variant, the following methodology reveals how it can be generally carried out, especially if they are using a DaaS model:

1. The Target Identification:
   This could be anybody or anything from a political opponent, to a business entity, or even just a common group of people. In this first phase, the Cyberattacker already has a plethora of tools at their disposal, which is available to the public. These are the following:

a. The social media profiles of the targeted victim.
b. Using what is known as "OSINT", which is an acronym that stands for "Open Source Intelligence". It can be technically defined as follows:

> Open-Source Intelligence (OSINT) is defined as intelligence produced by collecting, evaluating and analyzing publicly available information with the purpose of answering a specific intelligence question.
>
> *Source: https://www.sans.org/blog/what-is-open-source-intelligence/*

An example of OSINT can be seen in Figure 1.5.

2. The Hiring:
This is the step in which the Cyberattacker actually hires a DaaS agent, most likely getting from the Dark Web.
3. The Reconnaissance:
In this particular phase, the DaaS provider gathers much more detailed information about the victim, and from there, studies their vulnerabilities. After this, the DaaS agent then works closely with the Cyberattacker to pick how the Misinformation and Disinformation

*Figure 1.5* This is an example of OSINT.

**Source: https://www.shutterstock.com/image-photo/woman-working-documents-tablet-pc-notebook-585129634**

can be spread to cause the maximum amount of damage possible. This includes making use of the following:

a. Articles
b. Blog Posts
c. Videos
d. Social Media Posts
e. Social Media Accounts
f. Bots
g. Deep Fake Audio Recordings
h. Deep Fake Video Footages.

4. The Delivery:
Just like how the Cyberattacker will covertly deploy a Malicious Payload into the IT and Network Infrastructure of a business, in this regard, the Malicious Payload is the actual Disinformation and Misinformation content that is distributed and spread all across social media and other digital platforms.
5. The Exploitation:
In this particular phase, the DaaS agent manipulates the vulnerabilities of the victim that was discovered in the third step. This particularly involves totally hitting the victim with as much Misinformation and Disinformation that is possible, but in a highly targeted and selective fashion, much like how a Cyberattacker would move across laterally in an IT and Network Infrastructure. This phase can also be referred to technically as the "Persistent Phase" as well.
6. The Sustainment:
This is actually an extension of the last phase, and it is designed to keep the efforts ongoing in an effort to keep targeting the victim to inflict as much chaos and damage as possible. This will keep going on until the Cyberattacker who hired the DaaS agent literally says "stop".
7. The Actions:
In this very last phase of this entire cycle, the Cyberattacker and their respective DaaS agent will then attempt to further capitalize upon the damage that has been done to the victim, by launching the Threat Vectors into new and different directions, such as launching an Identity Theft (also known simply as "ID Theft") or Extortion Attacks directly against the victim.

As described, this particular kind of Misinformation and Disninformation Attack methodology can also inflict harm in other ways, which include the following:

- Reputational Damage:
This is the loss of customers, investors, and other key stakeholders.

- Legal Liability:
  Unfortunately, the victim can also be held liable for the spread of Misinformation and Disinformation, especially if a Court of Law sees the victim as contributing to the problem even more, even if they had no part whatsoever in it, from a technical standpoint.
- Disruptions:
  Just like in a Distributed Denial of Service (DDoS) and/or a Denial of Service (DoS) Attack, a DaaS Threat Variant can disrupt the victim's business operations by overloading its systems with plethora of Misinformation and Disinformation. This can lead to staggering losses in productivity and revenue for the business.

Chapter 2

# The effects of Generative AI on Misinformation and Disinformation

In the last chapter of this book, we provided an extensive overview of just what Misinformation and Disinformation are all about. Specifically, it covered the following topics:

- Misinformation and Disinformation
- The Subcategories of Misinformation and Disinformation
- The History of Misinformation and Disinformation
- Real-World Examples of Misinformation and Disinformation
- The Effects of Misinformation and Disinformation
- How Misinformation and Disinformation Are Evolving Into Cybersecurity
- How to Discern If You Are a Victim of a Misinformation and Disinformation Cyberattack
- How to Mitigate the Risks from Becoming a Victim of Misinformation and Disinformation
- Disinformation as a Service

A very common theme throughout the last chapter was that the spread of Misinformation and Disinformation is used heavily throughout the political seasons, especially as we are seeing right now. With the explosion of the social media platforms as the primary means by which people communicate, and the interconnectivity that they have with just about everything else in both the physical and virtual worlds, it is almost impossible to tell what is real and what is not.

This even holds true for its implications when it comes to Cybersecurity. The Cyberattackers of today are now resorting to this as their latest Threat Variant to launch against both businesses and individuals alike. It also uses the components of Social Engineering, which is yet another branch of Cybersecurity. Essentially, it uses covert, psychological techniques in order to prey upon the vulnerable emotions of the victim. Then once that trusting relationship has been established as best as possible, the Cyberattacker will then pounce, and move in for the proverbial "kill". This typically involves


DOI: 10.1201/9781003642374-2

the victim giving out the confidential and private information about themselves or about the company that they work for.

But as it was also eluded in the last chapter of this book, it's not simply the social media platforms, such as those of X, LinkedIn, YouTube, Facebook, Pinterest, and Instagram that are the primary catalysts for the spread of Misinformation and Disinformation. Another huge catalyst has been the dawn of Generative AI. For example, by using a platform like ChatGPT, or anything else similar, the Cyberattacker can create fake content that looks like the real thing. In this regard, the creation of Deepfakes is now being commonly used to lure in the victim.

As it was also reviewed in the last chapter, the use of Deepfakes is used heavily once again during the political seasons as well, especially when an election is coming, whether it is at the local level, state level, or even the federal level. In this regard, the Cyberattacker can create a fake video of the real candidates that running for whatever office that might be. In this instance, this fake video will then ask the voters to visit yet another phony website which will then ask them to donate to their specific campaign. But of course, any money that is donated will simply go to an offshore bank account located in a nation state threat actor, such as that of China, Russia, Iran, or even North Korea.

This chapter will provide an overview of how Deepfakes are created and deployed for the purposes of launching Misinformation and Disinformation campaigns. But first it is important at this point in this chapter to review the foundations of Generative AI, which is actually Artificial Intelligence in general, also known simply as "AI".

## AN OVERVIEW INTO ARTIFICIAL INTELLIGENCE

Believe it or not, Artificial Intelligence (in the remainder of this book, it will be referred to simply as "AI") has actually been around for quite a long time, going back as far as the 1950s. So while people of today look at it in sheer awe, there is nothing new to it at all. In the end, the ultimate goal of any AI system, tool, or model is to emulate the reasoning and thought processes of the human brain. But it is also very important to keep in mind that any AI system, model, or tool will never fully replicate the human at 100% capacity. At best, we may just reach just 0.000005% at most.

At this point, it is important to provide a technical definition of what AI is. It is as follows:

> Artificial intelligence (AI) makes it possible for machines to learn from experience, adjust to new inputs and perform human-like tasks. Most AI examples that you hear about today – from chess-playing computers to self-driving cars – rely heavily on deep learning and natural language processing. Using these technologies, computers can be trained

to accomplish specific tasks by processing large amounts of data and recognizing patterns in the data.

*Source: https://www.sas.com/en_us/insights/analytics/what-is-artificial-intelligence.html*

As one can see from the above definition, the main objective of AI is to have the ability to learn and project into the future by learning from past behaviors. This is heavily dependent upon the datasets that are fed into it, in order to derive the desired outputs. An illustration of AI can be seen in Figure 2.1.

As it was also mentioned just before at the start of this chapter, AI has a deep and rich history to it. We examine some of the key milestones in the next subsections of this chapter.

## The Turing test

The first well-known figure in the field of AI is that of Alan Turing. He is very often referred to as the "Father of Artificial Intelligence". Way back in 1936, he wrote a major, scientific paper entitled "On Computable Numbers". In this work, he actually lays down the concepts for what a computer is all about, and what its primary purposes are to be.

The basic idea for what his idea of a computer was based upon the premise that it had to be intelligent in some way, and serve a useful purpose. But at this point in time, it was very difficult to come up with an actual measure of what "intelligence" really was. Thus, this gave birth to what is now known as the "Turing Test".

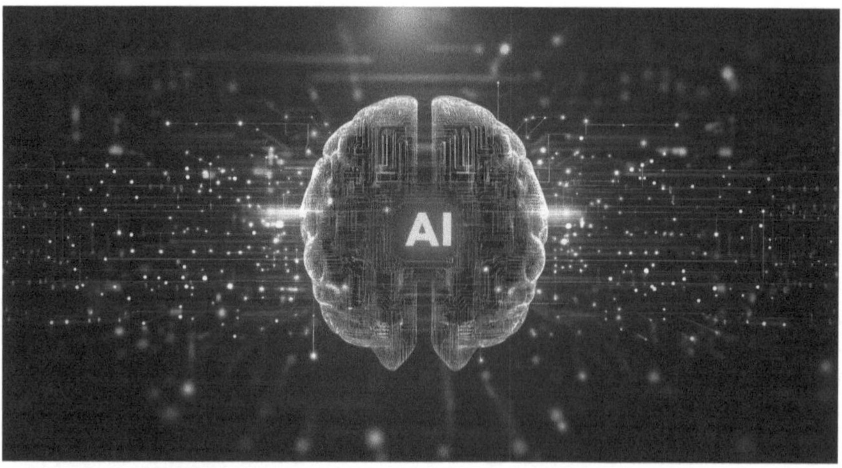


*Figure 2.1* This is an example of AI.

**Source: https://www.shutterstock.com/image-photo/digital-brain-circuit-ai-cocept-3d-2498421665**

In this scenario, there is a game with three players involved in it. Two of the participants are human beings, and the other is a computer. The third participant is the actual moderator. He or she will ask a series of open-ended questions to both participants, in an effort to determine which of the two of them is actually a human being. If a determination could not be made by asking these open-ended questions, it would then be assumed that the computer would be deemed as the "intelligent" entity.

## "Minds, brains, and programs"

The next major breakthrough to come after the Turing Test came with the publication of a scientific paper entitled "Minds, Brains, and Programs". This was written by the scientist known as John Searle, and was published in 1980. In this research paper, he formulated another model which closely paralleled the Turing Test, and it became known as the "Chinese Room Argument".

This paper that John Searle wrote also laid down the two types of AI that could potentially exist:

1. Strong AI:
   This is when a computer truly understands and is fully cognizant of what is transpiring around it. This area of AI is also technically known as "Artificial General Intelligence", or "AGI" for short.
2. Weak AI:
   This is a form of AI that is deemed to be not so strong in nature, by giving a very narrowed focus or set of tasks to work on.

## "A logical calculus of the ideas immanent in nervous activity"

The next major breakthrough to come in AI was a scientific paper entitled "A Logical Calculus of the Ideas Immanent In Nervous Activity". This was co-written by Warren McCulloch and Walter Pitts in 1943. The major premise of this paper was that logical deductions could explain the powers of the human brain, and was published in the "Bulletin of Mathematical Biophysics".

In this paper, McCulloch and Pitts make the hypothesis that the core functions of the human brain, in particular the neurons and synaptic activities that take place, can be fully explained by mathematical logical operators (e.g., And, Not).

## The origin story

The next major stepping stone in the world of AI came at Dartmouth University. There was a publication entitled "Study of Artificial Intelligence", and this was the first time that this term had ever been used. The exact nature of this project is as follows:

> The study is to proceed on the basis of the conjecture that every aspect of learning or any other feature of intelligence can be in principle be so precisely described that a machine can be made to simulate it. An attempt will thus be made to find out how to make machines use language, form abstractions and concepts, solve kinds of problems now reserved for humans, and improve themselves. We think that a significant advance can be made in one or more of these problems if a carefully selected group of scientists work on it together for a summer.
>
> *Source: "Artificial Intelligence Basics: A Non-Technical Introduction". Tom Tauli, Apress, 2019*

During this time frame, a computer program called the "Logic Theorist" was created and developed. The focus of this was to solve complex mathematical-based theorems from the publication known as the "Principia Mathematica". In order to create this programming language, an IBM 701 mainframe computer was also developed, making use of Machine Learning (which will be reviewed further in the next subsection of this chapter).

## Two newer theories on AI

Two major theories of AI also came about and they are as follows:

1. The need for symbolic systems:
   This would make heavy usage of computer-based logic, such as "If-Then-Else" statements.
2. The need for AI Systems to behave more like the human brain:
   This was the first known attempt to map the neurons in the brain, and their corresponding activities. This theory was developed by Frank Rosenblatt, but he renamed the neurons as "perceptrons".

Back in 1957, the first AI application was created, to do this, and it was called the "Mark I Perceptron". The computer that ran this particular program was fitted with two cameras to differentiate two separate images, whose scale was 20 × 20 pixels.

This AI application also served as the protégé for Neural Networks (which will also be reviewed in this chapter). One of the major flaws of this application is that it only had one layer of processing.

## The era of expert systems

During this timeframe, there were many other events that took place in the field of AI. One of these was the development of the Back Propagation

Technique. This is a technique which is assigned statistical weights for the inputs that go into a Neural Network system.

Another key development was the creation of what is known as the "Recurrent Neural Network", or "RNN" for short. This technique permits the connections in the AI system to move seamlessly through both the input and the output layers. Another key catalyst was the evolution of the microcomputer. This led to the development of what are known as "Expert Systems", which made heavy usage of symbolic logic.

One of the best examples of an Expert System was that of the "eXpert CONfigurer", or also known as the "XCON" for short. This was developed by John McDermott at the Carnegie Mellon University. The main purpose of this was to further advance the computer components, and in the end, the microcomputer developed at that time had about 2,500 rules (both mathematical and statistical based) that were incorporated into it. In a way, this was the forerunner to the Virtual Personal Assistants (VPAs) of Siri and Cortana which allow you to make choices.

### The evolution of deep learning

Finally, the 1980s saw the evolution of yet another new era in AI, known as "Deep Learning". It can be specifically defined as follows.

In simpler terms, this kind of system does not need already established mathematical or statistical algorithms in order to learn from the data that is fed into it. All it needs are certain permutations, and from there, it can literally learn on its own, and even make projections into the future.

## AN OVERVIEW OF MACHINE LEARNING

Machine Learning (also known as "ML", and referred to as such for the remainder of this book) plays a very important role in AI. In fact, it is deemed to be a subset of it, as are Neural Networks (which will be reviewed in more detail in the subsection), and Computer Vision (this is a branch of AI that tries to replicate the visual process of the human brain). Before we do a deeper dive into what Machine Learning is about, it is first important to give a technical definition of it, which is as follows:

> Machine learning (ML) is a branch of artificial intelligence (AI) focused on enabling computers and machines to imitate the way that humans learn, to perform tasks autonomously, and to improve their performance and accuracy through experience and exposure to more data.
>
> *Source: https://www.ibm.com/think/topics/machine-learning*

An image of ML is illustrated in Figure 2.2.

*Figure 2.2* This is an example of ML.

**Source: https://www.shutterstock.com/image-photo/machine-deep-learning-algorithms-artificial-intelligence-2491574645**

There are two main learning methods for ML models, which are as follows:

1. Semi-Structured Learning:
   This approach utilizes a hybrid approach of both Supervised and Unsupervised Learning. This is also known as "Self Supervised Machine Learning". In this instance, human intervention is still required to feed the datasets into the AI model, but the algorithms can still learn if the datasets are not categorized or classified. Also, with this kind of training, even Qualitative based datasets can be used for learning as well (which could include audio, images, video, etc.).
2. Reinforcement Learning:
   With this kind of approach, the AI model uses a system of "reward and punishment" in order for it to learn. For example, in these kinds of cases, a point system is used. If the AI model yields the correct outputs, it is awarded a certain numerical value. But if the output is skewed for whatever the reason may be, then this numerical value is reduced by a predetermined amount. This technique can be used to help train Digital Personas (chatbots with a human-like interface) to provide the right answers or course of action to a certain query that has been posed to it.

## The learning process of machine learning

Although the exact way that an ML model can trained will vary greatly of course upon the application that it is serving, the following is the general methodology in which it is carried out:

1. Ordering the Data Order:
   In this first step, you want to make sure that the data is cleaned, optimized, and organized in a logical format as much as possible. If there

are noticeable outliers or differences amongst the datasets, then the ML algorithms may recognize this as a legitimate pattern, which is obviously something that you do not want to happen.

2. Picking the Algorithm:
   In this second step, you will want to select the appropriate learning technique, as just reviewed in the last subsection of this chapter. Preference should always be geared toward Unsupervised Learning.
3. Training the Model:
   This is where the learning process for the AI model starts. It will look for various associations and relationships amongst the datasets so that the desired outputs can be formulated.
4. Evaluation of the Model:
   In this fourth step, after the training has been completed, you will then evaluate the results of the output. If it answers the query or the objective, then the training can be deemed to be successful. If not, you will have to go back and examine if there were any errors in the dataset that was ingested into the AI model.
5. Further Fine Tuning and Optimization:
   Once you have determined, the final step will then be make to sure that the AI model is always producing the desired outputs. This is where optimization and fine-tuning come into play. Also, this is where you want to have deployed Unsupervised Learning, if not, human intervention will be a huge time and resource drain.

## The Perceptron

One of the key components of any ML model (or for that matter, any AI model in general), is that of the Perceptron. Let us illustrate this with an example. For instance, the Central Processing Unit (CPU) is the main processing component of a computer. But if one were to equate this to the level of the brain, then it is called the "Neuron". The human brain consists of many neurons, and according to some scientific studies there are as many as almost 90 billion of them. Research has also shown that the Neuron is typically much slower than that of a CPU in the computer, but this is due to the fact that that there are so many of them, and the connections between the Perceptrons are even larger.

These connections are known as "Synapses", and interestingly enough, they work in a parallel fashion from one another, much like parallel processing in a computer. It should be noted that in the computer, the CPU is always active and the memory (such as the RAM) is a separate entity. But in the human brain, all of the Synapses are actually distributed evenly over its own network, and everything is connected and interlinked with one another.

A Perceptron can be technically defined as follows:

> A perceptron is the smallest element of a neural network. Perceptron is a single-layer neural network linear or a Machine Learning algorithm

> used for supervised learning of various binary classifiers. It works as an artificial neuron to perform computations by learning elements and processing them for detecting the business intelligence and capabilities of the input data.
>
> *Source: https://www.analytixlabs.co.in/blog/what-is-perceptron/*

It is the Perceptron that also forms the back for yet another branch of AI, which is called "Neural Networks". This is reviewed in the section of this chapter.

## AN OVERVIEW OF NEURAL NETWORKS

Along with the Perceptron, yet another key component of a Neural Network is that of the "Neuron". This is what provides the key basis for the Neural Network model. It can be technically defined as follows:

> Neurons are cells within the nervous system that transmit information to other nerve cells, muscle, or gland cells. Most neurons have a cell body, an axon, and dendrites. The cell body contains the nucleus and cytoplasm. The axon extends from the cell body and often gives rise to many smaller branches before ending at nerve terminals. Dendrites extend from the neuron cell body and receive messages from other neurons. Synapses are the contact points where one neuron communicates with another. The dendrites are covered with synapses formed by the ends of axons from other neurons.
>
> *Source: https://www.brainfacts.org/brain-anatomy-and-function/anatomy/2012/the-neuron*

When compared to ML, Neural Networks (also referred to as "NNs" and will be throughout the rest of this book) are different. For instance, it too needs data ingested into it for it to learn, but rather than taking the "Garbage In Garbage Out" that Machine Learning does, the Neurons are implemented so that the NN model can more or less learn on its own, and learn from any "mistakes" it may have made in the past. An example of this would be producing an output that did not reach the objective or a query that was posed to it.

An illustration of a Neuron can be seen in Figure 2.3.

### The artificial neural network

In more technical terms, the Neural Network that is deployed into an AI model is more commonly known as an "Artificial Neural Network", or "ANN" for short. The ANN consists of three major components:

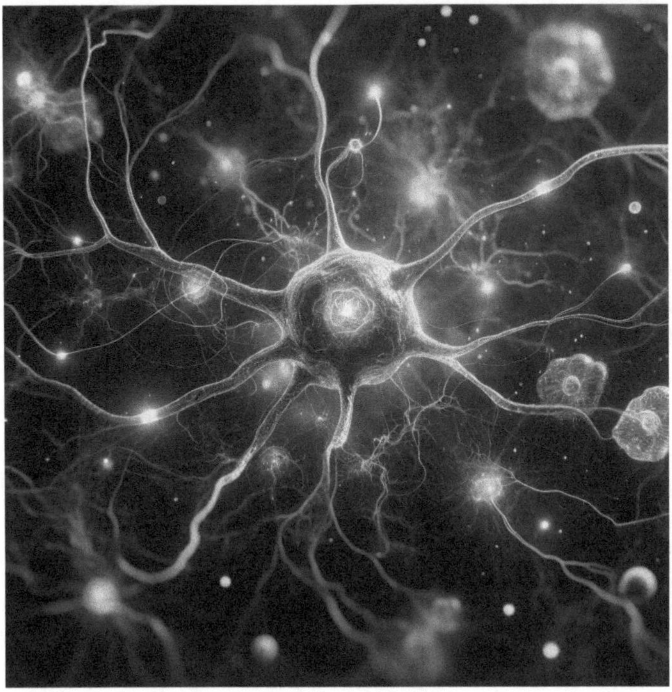

*Figure 2.3* This is an example of a neuron.

**Source: https://www.shutterstock.com/image-generated/neurons-firing-2469515741**

1. The Input Layer:
   This is also referred to as the "Input Layer". This is the first step for the ANN to start learning, and it is at this point that the data ingestion process actually starts.
2. The Hidden Layer:
   This is where the Neurons (also referred to technically as "Nodes") reside. It is important to note that each Neuron is assigned a particular Statistical Weight, which reflects how the datasets that have been ingested will be used not only for training purposes but also in creating the desired output. A simple definition of a Statistical Weight as it applies to ANNs is as follows:

   > Weights in a neural network are similar to the synaptic strengths in a biological brain. They are parameters that determine how strongly the output of one neuron influences the input of another. Weights control the impact of one neuron on another. During the training

process of a neural network, these weights are adjusted to minimize the error between the predicted output and the actual output.

*Source: https://www.askhandle.com/blog/neurons-and-weights-in-neural-networks*

3. The Output Layer:
   This is where the output is given, in the response to a query or objective that has been posed to it.

## The theoretical constructs of artificial neural networks

There are six major theoretical considerations of an ANN, which are as follows:

1. The activity of a Neuron in an ANN is deemed to be an "all or nothing" approach. This simply means the model is the entire way to predict the results of the output, or it is discarded in its entirety.
2. If any of the Neurons in the ANN have a statistical weighting of greater than 1, it then must be "excited" within a certain time period.
3. The only acceptable delays in an ANN system are those that are Synaptic based.
4. If any Neuron is deemed to be "inhibitory" in nature the only preventative action is that the actions of the Neurons be halted at a time in the ANN system.
5. The Neuron connections that are found in between the ANN do not, and should not change for any reason whatsoever.
6. The Neuron in the ANN system is actually composed of a binary format.

## The adaptive resonance theory

Another key concept of the Artificial Neural Network is known as the "Adaptive Resonance Theory", or "ART" for short. The goal of this AI theory is to create, develop, and deploy an ANN system with regard to recognizing patterns and classifying them. This is technically known as "Plasticity". Simply put, the ANN system becomes a central repository of everything that it has learned and will continue to learn in the future.

The ART Theory consists of three layers, which are as follows:

1. The Comparison Layer:
   A Binary Element is entered into the Neuron of the Comparison Layer.
2. The Recognition Layer:
   This is a variant of the "Classification Layer". The various inputs that it receives are mathematically derived from the "n" dimensional

weight vector "d". This is based on the property known as the "Lateral Inhibition Connection". This is where the output of each Neuron (denoted as "I") is connected via an "inhibitory" connection weighted matrix, denoted as follows:

3. The Gain and Reset Elements:
   These are which produce Scalar Outputs to all of the Neurons in the ANN system. A Scalar Output can be technically defined as follows:

> A scalar output for an artificial neural network is a single numerical value produced by the network as its final prediction, essentially a single number representing the result of the network's computation on the input data; this is typically used in regression tasks where the goal is to predict a continuous value like price, temperature, or distance.
>
> *Source: https://www.google.com/search?q=what+is+the+scalar+output+for+an+artificial+neural+network*

## The Cognitron

The Cognitron is a specialized type of ANN that has been designed for the deployment of Recognition Patterns. In order to do this, the Cognitron-based Neural Network makes total use of both the Inhibitory and Excitory Neurons. This kind of ANN is also considered to be a "Deep Learning" type of model.

An Inhibitory Neuron can be technically defined as follows:

> Inhibitory neurotransmitters are a specific type of neurotransmitter that plays a crucial role in decreasing the likelihood of an action potential (i.e., rapid rise of voltage across a cell membrane) being transmitted to another cell.
>
> *Source: https://www.osmosis.org/answers/inhibitory-neurotransmitters*

In other words, the human brain has a system of "checks and balances in place". These kinds of Neurons keep the brain in check, but keep the stimulation to an acceptable level.

An Excitory Neuron can be technically defined as follows:

> Excitatory Neurons "excite" the neuron and cause it to "fire off the message," meaning, the message continues to be passed along to the next cell. Examples of excitatory neurotransmitters include glutamate, epinephrine and norepinephrine.
>
> *Source: https://my.clevelandclinic.org/health/articles/22513-neurotransmitters*

### The Neocognitron

The last major component of an Artificial Neural Network is the Neocognitron. It can be technically defined as follows:

> A neocognitron is a type of artificial neural network, designed by Kunihiko Fukushima, that is specifically structured to recognize visual patterns with high tolerance to distortion, scaling, and translation, meaning it can identify objects even if they are slightly shifted or deformed in an image; it is considered a foundational model for hierarchical feature extraction in image recognition, often serving as inspiration for convolutional neural networks (CNNs) today.
>
> *Source: https://www.google.com/search?q=what+is+a+neocognitron*

With this, there are two groups of layers, which are composed of both Simple Cells and Multilayered Cells. There is also a three-tiered layer approach. This has been specifically designed so that the Neocognitron can overpower the various recognition issues that were not resolved by the Cognitron. Examples of this include images that are in the wrong kind of position or have any sort angular distortions.

## AN OVERVIEW OF GENERATIVE AI

Generative AI (also known as just "Gen AI") is deemed to be one of the newest fields from within AI in itself. Although the term may be new to most of us, it is actually deemed to be an "offspring" of both ML and NNs. Generative AI can be technically defined as follows:

> Generative artificial intelligence, also known as generative AI or gen AI for short, is a type of AI that can create new content and ideas, including conversations, stories, images, videos, and music. It can learn human language, programming languages, art, chemistry, biology, or any complex subject matter. It reuses what it knows to solve new problems.
>
> *Source: https://aws.amazon.com/what-is/generative-ai/*

An illustration of Gen AI can be seen in Figure 2.4.

So as one can see from the above definition, what separates Gen AI from the other branches of AI are the kind of outputs that it can create. This is reviewed in more detail in the next subsection of this chapter.

### The Outputs that are created from Generative AI

The Outputs that can be created from Generative AI were reviewed at a high level in the last section. In this section, we do a deeper dive into them. The Outputs are as follows:

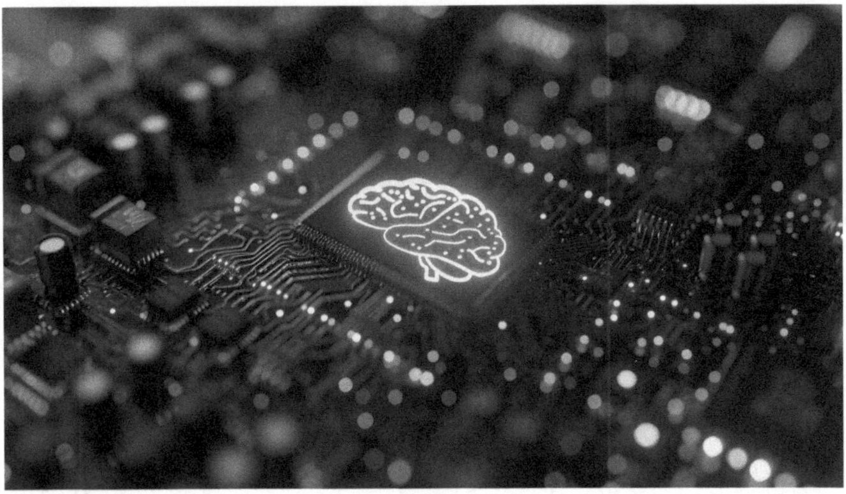

*Figure 2.4* This is an example of Gen AI.

**Source: https://www.shutterstock.com/image-photo/concept-mother board-picture-brain-technology-ram-2422220481**

1. The Text Generation:
   In this instance, the Output that is created in a tool like ChatGPT is merely a content-based one. The specific algorithms that are used to formulate the Outputs are what is known as "The Transformer Architecture". This forms the constructs for the GPT3 and GPT4 Algorithms. It can be technically defined as follows:

   > The GPT algorithm, short for Generative Pre-trained Transformer algorithm ... [it[is designed to generate coherent and contextually relevant text based on input prompts.
   >
   > *Source: https://itexus.com/glossary/gpt-algorithm/#gref*

   It should be noted here that a prime catalyst for the GPT3 and GPT4 Algorithms are the prompts that the end user creates when trying to get an answer (also the Output) to their specific query. For instance, when you make use of Google as a Search Engine, you simply enter some keywords or even a simple question. In response, and for that matter in just a matter of seconds, pages of resources come up that you can peruse through. But, these are not a specific answer to your query, rather, Google is letting you decide what is best. But with the GPT3 and GPT4 Algorithms, the end user is actually getting a specific answer to their particular query. But given the ultra sophistication of them, the end user has to construct a query that will yield the specific answer (also the Output) that they are looking for.

In other words, when using a tool such as ChatGPT, the more refined your query is, the better the result will be from your generated Outputs. But it is important to keep in mind here that "Prompt Engineering" is not a subject that can be learned from an online course, rather, it is learned strictly through rote practice and repetition. The typical application for this is in content generation, such as creating a blog or an article of sorts. It can even be used to further check for the integrity of the grammar and syntax of the sentences for content that has already been created.

2. The Image Generation:
For this kind of Output to be specifically created, Deep Learning Models are heavily utilized from within the realms of Generative AI. What makes something like ChatGPT different from AI is that actual images can be used as a Dataset to feed into the model. This can then be used to create an image to serve as the Output. This kind of Dataset can also be viewed as a "Qualitative" based one because it is not just a Dataset based upon pure numerical values. To create the images as Outputs, ChatGPT also makes use of what is known as "General Adversarial Networks" or "GANs" for short. In this case, a "Generator" is used to create the actual images based upon what it has been trained on, and then the "Discriminator" is then used to determine if the created image is actually a fake or not. This is actually an iterative process that keeps repeating itself until an image is ultimately created that matches the need of the specific query. The applications for this are very numerous, as long as there is an image that needs to be created.
3. The Audio Generation:
In this kind of scenario, rather than creating a text or an image for the needed Output, an audio file is created as the Output. But what makes this different is that if the end user submits a specific query to ChatGPT, the Output does not have to be an actual text. Rather, if the end user specifies that the Output should be in the form of an audio file, then that is what ChatGPT will produce.
4. The Video Generation:
This kind of Output that is generated and created by ChatGPT is actually deemed to be the most complex in terms of the processes that are involved with it. One of the primary reasons for this is that in this particular instance, there have to be many videos that have to be fed into whatever Generative AI model that is used to compute the video-based Outputs. They also must be of the correct nature, if not, the Generative AI model will have to "guess" what the missing parts of the Output will need to be. Although this entire process can transpire within minutes if not seconds, it can by its very nature take a lot of both computing and processing resources in order for the right kind of Outputs to be created. But despite their complexity, video-based Outputs are also deemed to be the most sophisticated, because they can make use of

both Computer Vision and Facial Recognition, and the Outputs that are yielded from this can serve a wide variety of market applications ranging from Forensics to Law Enforcement.

## Natural language processing

A very key component of Generative AI is what is known as "Natural Language Processing" also known as "NLP" for short, and this will be used throughout the rest of this book. A technical definition of NLP is as follows:

> Natural language processing (NLP) is a branch of artificial intelligence (https://www.sas.com/en_us/insights/analytics/what-is-artificial-intelligence.html) that helps computers understand, interpret and manipulate human language. NLP draws from many disciplines, including computer science and computational linguistics, in its pursuit to fill the gap between human communication and computer understanding.
>
> *Source: https://www.sas.com/en_us/insights/analytics/what-is-natural-language-processing-nlp.html*

In other words, NLP literally acts as the bridge between the human voice and the computer that is attempting to process it. A perfect example of this is what is known as the "Digital Personality", and this is illustrated in Figure 2.5.

*Figure 2.5* This is an example of a digital personality.

**Source: https://www.shutterstock.com/image-photo/online-beauty-video-broadcast-vlogger-beautiful-1859941942**

It is important to note that there are a number of key concepts that are associated with NLP, and they are as follows, and are reviewed in the next subsection of this chapter.

## The concept of the N-gram

1. Tokenization:
   This is the process where a sentence is broken into its individual words. These single words then become technically what is known as "Tokens". An example of this is below:
   "I love Artificial Intelligence"
   The above is the actual human voice.
   ["I"] ["love"] ["Artificial"] ["Intelligence"]
   The above is the "Tokenization", and each of the individuals thus becomes a single "Token".
   "Tokenization" is primarily used so that large and complex human sentences can be broken down so that the NLP Model and the corresponding Algorithms can process them efficiently and effectively.

In the world of "Tokenization", another concept called the "N-grams" are also used. They are simply a mathematical sequence of the total number of "N Tokens" in any given sentence. They can be anything such as the actual words, spaces, punctuation marks, any type or kind of alphanumeric characters, phonemes, etc. There are different kinds of these, and they are as follows:

1. The Unigram:
   This is also known technically as the "1-Gram", as its name implies. These are merely mathematical representations of each single word in a given sentence. So in this example:
   "I love Artificial Intelligence"
   ["I"] ["love"] ["Artificial"] ["Intelligence"]
   Each word in quotation marks thus becomes one, singular "Unigram".
2. The Bigrams:
   This is also known technically as the "2-Gram", as its name implies. These are merely mathematical representations of two words (in a pair" in a given sentence. So in this example:
   "I love Artificial Intelligence"
   ["I" "love"] ["Artificial" "Intelligence"]
   Each two-pair word in quotation marks thus becomes one, dual-level "Bigram".
3. The Trigram:
   This is also known technically as the "3-Gram", as its name implies. These are merely mathematical representations of each three-word combination in a given sentence. So in this example:
   ["I" "love"] ["Artificial" "Intelligence"] ["very" "much"]

Every three-word combination in quotation marks thus becomes one, trilevel "Trigram".

4. The N-Gram in Language Modeling:
   This is a specialized Algorithm that is used to compute the Statistical Probability of what a particular word actually means in the entire context of a sentence.
5. The N-Gram in Text-Based Classification:
   This is a specialized Algorithm in order to discern if a word has a positive or negative connotation to it. For example, in the examples up above, the word "love" represents a positive connotation, but if the word "despise" were to be substituted for it, it would thus have a negative connotation to it. This kind of Algorithm is heavily used in a subfield of Generative AI which is called "Sentiment Analysis". This too can be technically defined as follows:

   > Sentiment analysis is the process of analyzing digital text to determine if the emotional tone of the message is positive, negative, or neutral.
   >
   > *Source: https://aws.amazon.com/what-is/sentiment-analysis/*

6. The N-Gram and its Limitations:
   In this situation, it is quite possible that an "N-Gram" may lose its ability to determine the context of a word, if the sentence is very long and convoluted. For example, in this sentence:
   "I love Artificial Intelligence, but I hate learning how to code".
   The Algorithm will quickly pick up on the connotation of "love", but the chances that it will for the word "hate" becomes lesser. Also, it is important to note here that if the Algorithm is trying to decipher the context of individual words in a foreign language, it will not be able to do so unless the Generative AI Model has been specifically fed Datasets of that particular language into it.
7. The N-Gram in Out of Vocabulary Words:
   The acronym for this kind of Algorithm is known as the "OOV". In this case, the Algorithm may not actually recognize a particular word in a given sentence, thus it will assign what is known as a "Random Token" that is unique only to that particular word.
8. The N-Gram and Smoothing:
   This kind of Algorithm will actually try to ascertain both the meaning and the contexts of words in a given sentence if there are too many of them in which connotations cannot be understood by the Generative AI Model.

## The variational autoencoder

These are also technically known as the "VAEs" for short. This is also a variation of the Generative AI Model, and this kind of setup primarily makes use of what are known as "Autoencoders" and "Probabilistic Modeling".

These kinds of Generative AI Models are designed to not only capture what they have learned in the past, but also apply that knowledge in making future predictions and computing the various Outputs to the queries that are submitted to the Model.

The VAE can be technically defined as follows:

> Variational autoencoders (VAEs) are generative models used in machine learning (ML) to generate new data in the form of variations of the input data they're trained on. In addition to this, they also perform tasks common to other autoencoders, such as denoising.
>
> *Source: https://www.ibm.com/think/topics/variational-autoencoder*

This kind of Generative AI Mechanism consists of the following components:

1. The Encoder:
   This takes the Datasets that not only the Generative AI Model has been trained on, but what has been fed into recently. Unlike the other types and kinds of "Encoders" that have been reviewed previously in this book, this one does not represent the Data as a fixed length.
2. Latent Space:
   'This is a "space" that has been specifically allocated into the Generative AI Model for those Datasets that have been deemed to be of a "Secondary Nature", and will not be used in the initial round of training for the Model. Rather, they will be called upon in the future if more Datasets are needed to further optimize the Generative AI Model.
3. The Reparameterization "Trick":
   In this kind of scenario, rather than having the Generative AI Model learn directly from the Datasets, hypothetical ones are created instead in order for it to train on. It should be noted that these kinds of Datasets are also technically referred to as "Synthetic Data." This can be technically defined as follows:

   > Synthetic data is non-human-created data that mimics real-world data. It is created by computing algorithms and simulations based on generative artificial intelligence technologies. A synthetic data set has the same mathematical properties as the actual data it is based on, but it does not contain any of the same information. Organizations use synthetic data for research, testing, new development, and machine learning research. Recent innovations in AI have made synthetic data generation efficient and fast but have also increased its importance in data regulatory concerns.
   >
   > *Source: https://aws.amazon.com/what-is/synthetic-data/*

4. The Decoder:
   This functionality of the Generative AI Model will take a sample from the "Secondary Dataset" as just described, and attempt to actually

"map" it back to the original Datasets. In simpler terms, this is an attempt to use these "Secondary Datasets" to fill any voids or gaps that exist in the primary Datasets upon which the Generative AI Model trains upon.

5. The Loss Function:
   The VAE is designed to be trained upon those Datasets that have a lower Statistical Probability of being used by the Generative AI Model. There are two key concepts that are associated with this, and they are as follows:
   - The Reconstruction:
     This functionality actually measures how well the "Synthetic Datasets" actually correlate with the "Primary Datasets" that are stored in the Generative AI Model.
   - The Regularization:
     This functionality helps to ensure that the "Synthetic Datasets" that have been produced and utilized are actually void of any gaps or holes that could potentially exist. The primary reason for doing this is that since these kinds of Datasets are "manufactured data" and really have no real-world value attached to them, they must, as much as possible look like the real thing.
6. The Generation and the Interpolation:
   Once the Generative AI Model has actually been deemed to be fully trained, the VAE can then actually create new Datasets (which are actually still "Synthetic" in nature, and from there, send it off to the "Decoder" in order to confirm and validate that indeed these new types of Datasets can actually be subsequently used by the Generative AI Model not just for the purposes of training, but for also computing the Outputs as well.

## The general adversarial network

These are also technically known as "GANs". The GAN is actually a Machine Learning Model of sorts, in which new Datasets can be created from which it has learned previously before. However, the GAN is not deemed to be as sophisticated as the VAE, as it can only produce newer kinds of Datasets from the sources that it has been fed information and data from. Whereas with the VAE, given the extra number of components that it possesses, can produce newer types of Datasets from other sources of information and data that it has not trained previously upon.

The GAN can be technically defined as follows:

> A generative adversarial network (GAN) is a deep learning architecture. It trains two neural networks to compete against each other to generate more authentic new data from a given training dataset. For instance, you can generate new images from an existing image database

or original music from a database of songs. A GAN is called adversarial because it trains two different networks and pits them against each other. One network generates new data by taking an input data sample and modifying it as much as possible. The other network tries to predict whether the generated data output belongs in the original dataset. In other words, the predicting network determines whether the generated data is fake or real. The system generates newer, improved versions of fake data values until the predicting network can no longer distinguish fake from original.

*Source: https://aws.amazon.com/what-is/gan/*

The GAN consists of two primary components, which are as follows:

1. The Generator:
   Although limited in sophistication to the "Encoder" (reviewed in the last section), the Generator still actually produces newer types and kinds of Datasets that closely parallel the Datasets that have been fed previously into the Generative AI Model. But it should be noted here that at the initial outset, the Datasets that have been produced by the "Generator" mano not closely match the Datasets that the Generative AI Model has been fed, and trained upon.
2. The Discriminator:
   In technical terms, this component of the GAN is also known as the "Binary Classifier", in the sense that it can take the "real" Datasets that have been ingested into the Generative AI Model and the produced Datasets and from there, try to ascertain what is actually "fake" amongst the Datasets. It should be noted here that this is actually an iterative process that keeps on cycling through the GAN so that eventually the reproduced or "fake" Datasets will actually look like the real Datasets.

The training is the actual iterative process just described. But, once this process is actually deemed to have been completed, the permutations that have been fed into the "Generator" are further modified, based on the number of cycles that are needed for the "fake" Datasets to closely mirror and correlate with the real Datasets. While this can possibly be done on an automated basis, it is highly advised human intervention is also required at this point.

Finally, once the iterative process comes to a point of completion, this is technically known as the "State of Equilibrium". This simply means that it is, from the standpoint of Statistics, for the Discriminator to distinguish what is the "fake" and real data, even on a granular level. Further, it is at this point, that how and where the permutations should be modified needs to be taken into serious consideration.

## The diffusion model

Another recent advancement that has been made in Generative AI is that of the "Diffusion Model". It is sophisticated in the sense that it actually draws upon the concepts of Quantum Mechanics and Computer Science. For example, whatever level of "noise" that may actually exist in the Datasets (whether they are "fake" or real) can actually be converted into newer forms of Datasets, that can also be ingested into the Generative AI Model. On a macro level, this process is done by actually Reverse Engineering the point where at "noise" is first introduced in the Datasets.

The Diffusion Model can be technically defined as follows:

> Diffusion models are generative models used primarily for image generation and other computer vision tasks. Diffusion-based neural networks are trained through deep learning to progressively "diffuse" samples with random noise, then reverse that diffusion process to generate high-quality images.
>
> *Source: https://www.ibm.com/think/topics/diffusion-models*

## THE DALL-E-2

One of the cutting-edge solutions that have occurred in Generative AI, and especially that of ChatGPT is having the functionality of taking a query that was submitted by, normal human language, and actually converting that directly to an image, as the Output (if this has been created by the end user). The specific Algorithm that drives is the "DALL-E-2", and it too was developed by OpenAI as well.

It can be technically defined as follows:

> DALL-E-2 is an AI system that can create realistic images and art from a description in natural language.
>
> *Source: https://openai.com/index/dall-e-2/*

How this process actually works is the focal point of this section, and it as follows:

1. The Inputs:
   This is where the DALL-E-2 will take either an audio or a textual description of the image that is to be created. From there, it is then transferred into the Generative AI Model.
2. The Encoding:
   This is where the query that has been submitted (either via text or audio) is then further processed by the DALL-E-2 Algorithm. At this point, it actually makes use of a specialized kind of Neural Network

called the "Contrastive Language – Image Pre Training" also referred to technically as the "CLIP". From here, the input that is provided by the end user becomes a mathematical-based, vector representation of it. The goal here at this step is to capture as much as possible the "semantic meaning" of the input.

3. The Conversion:
   At this point in the process, the vector-based representations that have been produced by the "CLIP" are directed yet into another Algorithm which is called the "Prior". This too is a Diffusion Model (or it can also be an Autoregressive one, based upon the requirements that have been set forth onto the Generative AI Model), and this is deemed to be the first stage at where the submitted input actually starts getting converted over into an image of sorts. To do this, the "Prior" makes use of a Statistical based, Probabilistic Model.
4. The Generation:
   It is at this stage, after going through the required number of iterations in the last step, that whatever has been produced by the "Prior" Algorithm is now thus transmitted over to the "Diffusion Decoder". This is where it is used to convert all of the mathematical vectors that have been computed in the last step now become recognizable images, that can in the end be used as an Output in order to satisfy the query that has been submitted to the Generative AI Model.

## THE RISE OF DEEPFAKES

The concept of Deepfakes was introduced earlier in this chapter. To review, a technical definition of it is as follows:

> A deepfake refers to a specific kind of synthetic media where a person in an image or video is swapped with another person's likeness.
>
> *Source: https://mitsloan.mit.edu/ideas-made-to-matter/deepfakes-explained*

In other words, the likeness of somebody is maliciously replicated using the Generative AI in order to launch both Phishing and Social Engineering Attacks. Also, as it was mentioned throughout this entire chapter, they are used heavily during the election seasons, whether it is at the local, state, or Federal levels. In the next subsection of this chapter, we examine how the Deepfake is actually constructed.

### How it is done

In the end, Deepfakes uses only two types of Generative AI algorithms, which are as follows:

- The Generator
- The Discriminator

As it was reviewed in detail in this chapter, the Generator creates a data set based on the desired output, such as creating the initial fake video. The Discriminator then analyzes how realistic the fake video is. This is a continual, iterative process that allows for the Generator to improve at creating realistic, but fake video, and the Discriminator in turn becomes that much better at detecting any kind or types of flaws for the Generator to correct.

The summation of the Generator and the Discriminator models creates the Generative Adversarial Network (or "GAN"), which was also reviewed in this chapter. The GAN makes A GAN uses what is known as "Deep Learning". This can be technically defined as follows:

> Deep learning is a subset of machine learning that uses multilayered neural networks, called deep neural networks, to simulate the complex decision-making power of the human brain. Some form of deep learning powers most of the artificial intelligence (AI) applications in our lives today.
>
> *Source: https://www.ibm.com/think/topics/deep-learning*

The GAN is primarily used to detect and recognize undiscernible patterns in the real video and then it uses the patterns to create the fakes. When creating a deepfake photograph, a GAN system views photographs of the target from an array of angles to capture all the details and perspectives. When creating a Deepfake video, the GAN views the datasets from various angles and analyzes the following:

- The Behavior of the real person.
- The Movement of the real person.
- The Speech Patterns of the real person.

All of this information is then processed through the Discriminator many times to make the fake video look as real as possible.

## The use cases of deepfakes

There are three main areas where Deepfakes can be, and in fact, are used quite widely. They are as follows:

1. The Deepfake Videos:
   A specialized form of a Deepfake Autoencoder is used to further study the content of the real video in order to fully understand its relevant attributes. This can include the Facial Expressions and as well as the Body Language of the real person that is being replicated into a fake

version. Once this has been done, the algorithms then superimposes these discovered attributes onto the real and authentic video.

2. The Deepfake Audio:
   In this particular instance, the GAN clones the actual audio of the real person's voice. From there, a model is then created which is based upon the vocal patterns of the real person. From there, the GAN makes a Generative AI model that will make the fake voice say anything the creator wants.
3. The Deepfake Lips:
   This actually refers to "Lip Syncing", such as when it looks like a singer is actually singing, but in reality, they are just moving or "synching" their lips accordingly. But, when it comes to the actual Deepfake, the voice of the real person is mapped according to the tempo of the fake video, so it makes it look like the Deepfake video is actually speaking the words. This is all done by what is known as "Recurrent Neural Networks", or "RNNs" for short. It can be technically defined as follows:

   > A recurrent neural network or RNN is a deep neural network trained on sequential or time series data to create a machine learning (ML) model that can make sequential predictions or conclusions based on sequential inputs.
   >
   > *Source: https://www.ibm.com/think/topics/recurrent-neural-networks*

## The technologies behind the deepfake

There are a number of different Generative AI powered technologies that can create Deepfakes of all kinds and types. They are as follows:

1. The GAN:
   This has been extensively reviewed throughout this chapter, and to summarize, it makes use of the Autoencoder and Decoder to produce a Deepfake, of any kind of content, such as audio, video, image, and text.
2. The CNN:
   This is an acronym that stands for "Convoluted Neural Networks". It can be technically defined as follows:

   > Convolutional neural networks use three-dimensional data for image classification and object recognition tasks.
   >
   > *Source: https://www.ibm.com/think/topics/convolutional-neural-networks*

   This kind of Generative AI model is used to analyze the succinct patterns in the visual data that are present, or difficult to detect. They primarily use facial recognition and movement tracking.

3. The NLP:
As also reviewed earlier in this chapter, this is an acronym that stands for "Natural Language Processing". In summary, it is used for analyzing the attributes of a real person's speech and then from there, generate original but fake text that incorporates those specific attributes.
4. The HPC:
This is an acronym that stands for "High Performance Computing". It can be technically defined as follows:

> High-performance computing (HPC) is the art and science of using groups of cutting edge computer systems to perform complex simulations, computations, and data analysis out of reach for standard commercial compute systems available.

In other words, HPC provides the required computing power that Deepfakes require.

## The legality of deepfakes

Apart from the technical aspects of Deepfakes just examined in this chapter, the next question that often gets asked is the following: "Are they legal?" At the current time, there are no Federal Laws that make the development and deployment of Deepfakes illegal. But, there are three unique circumstances in which it would be deemed illegal if they are used:

- Child Pornography
- Defamation against the victim
- Any kind or type of hate-related speech that causes a direct impact on the victim.

However, there are about forty states in which there is legislation pending that would make Deepfakes illegal if they are passed. There is also legislation that is pending at the Federal Government level and a sampling of them is as follows:

1. The DEFIANCE Act:
This is an acronym that stands for "Disrupt Explicit Forged Images and Non-Consensual Edits". If these piece of legislation were to be passed, it would technically become the first Federal Law of its kind to protect victims of deepfakes. Further, it allows for the file lawsuits against the creators of the Deepfake in question if they did not get explicit permission from the victim to create the Deepfake in the first place.
2. The Preventing Deepfakes of Intimate Images Act:
Joe Morelle, a member of the United States House of Representatives, introduced the bill for this piece of legislation in May of 2003. It is

intended to criminalize the sharing of Deepfakes to protect individuals from the Generative AI powered creation and distribution of them that have not been authorized.

3. The Take It Down Act:
   This is an acronym that stands for the "Tools to Address Known Exploitation by Immobilizing Technological Deepfakes on Websites and Networks". If this piece of legislation were to be passed, it would make it completely criminal to publish or threaten a pornographic-based Deepfake. Also, it would mandate that the major social media platforms (such as LinkedIn, X, Facebook, Instagram, and Pinterest) to remove a Deppfake within a 48 hour time span after receiving a valid request from a victim.
4. The Deepfakes Accountability Act:
   This bill was introduced by Yvette Clarke and Glenn Ivey, both members of the House of Representatives in September of 2023. If this were to become actual legislation, this would require the creators of Deepfakes to include a digital-based watermark onto it, so people can see that whatever is produced is not the real thing.

## Revealing clues of a deepfake

Although they can be difficult to detect, there are subtle clues that a Deepfake can reveal to prove that they are not for real. Here they are:

- Any kind or type of positioning of the face.
- Any kind or type of unnatural bodily movement.
- Any kind or type of unnatural coloring that is present in the external environment.
- Any kind of or type of video that looks very unusual is magnified.
- Any kind or type of break ups in the audio.
- A person that does not blink at all.
- Any kind or type of the most minute deviations in the reflected light in the eyes of the person that is in the Deepfake.
- Any kind or type of mismatch in the actual coloring of the skin.
- Glasses that either have no glare or have too much of it. Also, if the angle of the glare stays the same consistently through the content of the Deepfake.

Finally, a Deepfake is illustrated in Figure 2.6.

*Figure 2.6* This is an example of a deepfake.

**Source: https://www.shutterstock.com/image-photo/positive-sports woman-working-out-next-swimming-2206438703**

Chapter 3

# The effects of social engineering on Misinformation and Disinformation

As one can see throughout this entire book thus far, the primary theme of it has been both Misinformation and Disinformation. We have examined from numerous perspectives, but especially from both the Cybersecurity and Non Cybersecurity perspectives. Also, the various types and kinds of Threat Variants are associated with both Misinformation and Disinformation, but the one that was reviewed extensively was about Deepfakes. In this chapter, we look at yet another Threat Variant that arises from Misinformation and Disinformation. This is known technically as "Social Engineering".

It can also be technically defined as follows:

> Social engineering is the term used for a broad range of malicious activities accomplished through human interactions. It uses psychological manipulation to trick users into making security mistakes or giving away sensitive information.
>
> Social engineering attacks happen in one or more steps. A perpetrator first investigates the intended victim to gather necessary background information, such as potential points of entry and weak security protocols, needed to proceed with the attack. Then, the attacker moves to gain the victim's trust and provide stimuli for subsequent actions that break security practices, such as revealing sensitive information or granting access to critical resources.
>
> *Source: https://www.imperva.com/learn/application-security/social-engineering-attack/*

The above definition can be illustrated with a simple example. Suppose there is a business, and it is called "Company XYZ". The CEO has an administrative assistant, with whom he has had a very long and trusting relationship, spanning 20 years. But all of a sudden, she receives a call from someone claiming to be a third supplier of theirs. Rather than trying to launch straight


DOI: 10.1201/9781003642374-3

into a Business Email Compromise (BEC) Attack, this person calls periodically, on an infrequent basis. Over this course of time, this person (who is now actually a Cyberattacker) develops a close, and confidential relationship with this particular administrative assistant. But, it is important to note at this point that there is no physical contact made whatsoever between the two of them.

All of the communication that takes place between the two of them is done in the virtual world, for example, in Microsoft Teams, SMS Texting, Email, etc. In fact, the Cyberattacker never even plans to make, direct physical contact with the administrative assistant. Over time, the Cyberattacker starts to develop a strong sense of empathy toward the administrative assistant. This can include any kind or type of situation that the administrative assistant encounters in the workplace that she is currently in.

Then over time, this particular administrative assistant actually starts to develop a certain set of feelings for this Cyberattacker that she is conversing with. Then, once these feelings have been strongly solidified, the Cyberattacker then moves into the proverbial "kill". At this point, he then claims he needs the login credentials to one of the most sensitive databases in the company. Without giving it a second thought, the administrative gives everything that the Cyberattacker wants or claims what he really needs. Then guess what happens next? The Cyberattacker now has all of the keys to the kingdom, and can now do pretty much everything and anything that they want to. This can range from launching a covert Data Exfiltration Attack to even launching Extortion Attacks. Or at this point, they can even launch that BEC Email Compromise Attack. This can be technically defined as follows:

> Business Email Compromise (BEC) is a type of cyber-attack in which an attacker impersonates a trusted individual, such as a senior executive or a vendor, to trick an organization or individual into divulging sensitive information or transferring funds. This attack vector has become increasingly prevalent in recent years, resulting in significant financial losses for businesses of all sizes.
>
> In a typical BEC attack, the attacker conducts extensive research to learn about their target organization, including its key personnel, vendors, and business processes. They will then use this information to craft convincing emails that appear to come from a trusted source, often with a sense of urgency or importance, in order to prompt the recipient to take immediate action.
>
> *Source: https://darktrace.com/cyber-ai-glossary/business-email-compromise*

This entire process is illustrated in Figure 3.1:

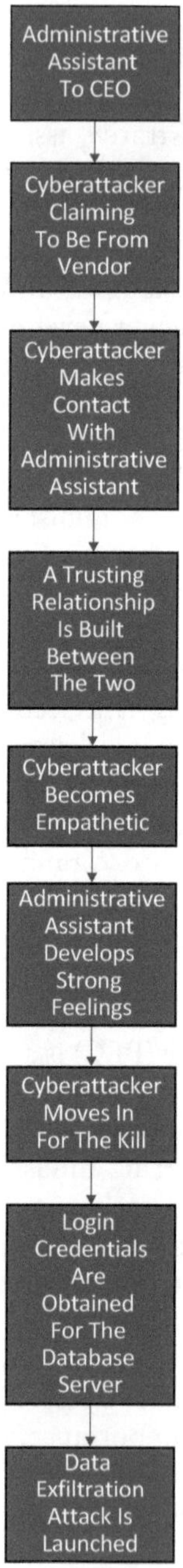


*Figure 3.1* An example of a BEC Attack.

## THE DIFFERENT WAYS IN WHICH A SOCIAL ENGINEERING ATTACK CAN BE LAUNCHED

The example that was portrayed in the last section of this chapter is just one way that a Social Engineering Attack can be launched. But with regards to this, there are two very important aspects to keep in mind:

- A good Social Engineering Attack takes time to launch, after all, as it was illustrated in the last example, the Cyberattacker needs to develop both a personal and professional relationship with the victim.
- A Social Engineering Attack is deemed to be officially launched when the Cyberattacker officially preys upon the vulnerable, emotional state of the victim, and directly asks for login credentials or something of a similar nature.

The list below examines other ways in which the Cyberattacker can prey upon the emotional state of their particular victim, in order to make the move in which to launch a Social Engineering Attack:

1. The Liking:
   In this instance, the Cyberattacker appears to be trustworthy and/or even attractive in nature. To build up a stronger rapport, the Cyberattacker may try to share similar interests with those of their victim.
2. The Reciprocity:
   In this case, the Cyberattacker tries to offer advice, or some kind of other personal service victim to their victim so that they feel obliged to give something back.
3. The Commitment:
   In this instance, the Cyberattacker makes their victim agree to do small things for them before moving on to the bigger things. The Cyberattacker may also have their victim agree to take a specific action before the risks become known to them.
4. The Social Proof:
   In this case, the Cyberattacker will make use of social networking on social media platforms by making false statements that the victim's online friends approve of a certain action that has been conducted.
5. The Authority:
   It is human nature for people to believe that anything said by someone in a position of authority is automatically true, without further questioning its validity or double-checking the sources from where the information and/or data came. Thus in this instance, this is what the Cyberattacker exactly pretends to do. Thus, the Cyberattacker will use phrases such as "according to experts", etc. to convince their victim target to agree to something that they would normally not do.

## THE HISTORY OF SOCIAL ENGINEERING

Since Social Engineering involves human contact (whether it is direct or even non-direct), and preying upon the emotions and the vulnerable state of people, it has a long history in terms of its actual origination. Although it is still quite sketchy to fully confirm, in this section of this chapter, we will provide an overview in order to give you an idea, of just how long it goes back.

1. After the French Revolution:
   Once this particular time period was over in France, the prisoners of war that were held in France spread false claims that they were valets for the French noblemen. Not only that, they had also sent out letters which also falsely stated that they knew where a certain treasure was located that was hidden by the French Noblemen. They would provide a map, and in turn, would want some kind of compensation and better treatment in their holding facilities. This is actually an example of Reciprocity, as it was just reviewed.
2. The Nobleman Located in Europe:
   This is the almost same kind of Social Engineering Attack that was just described. But, rather than having it isolated to just the French Noblemen, it now included all of the Noblemen located throughout the entire European Continent.
   In the letter that was written and sent to all of these Noblemen, they claimed to be a European nobleman who had been imprisoned under the false pretenses. This letter asked the European Noblemen would ask for enough money to secure their release.
3. The Times in Nigeria:
   When one thinks of this particular country, unfortunately, the thoughts of terrorism and Phishing emails very often come to mind. In fact, this is how Social Engineering actually came into emergence into Cybersecurity. For example, fake documents with a malicious payload were attached to them. Then from here, the sender of the Phishing email pretended to be a Nigerian prince once making false claims there was money locked away and that it needed to be transferred to the victim's own bank account. If the victim agreed to this particular scam, the fictitious Nigerian Prince would then share any extra money with the victim. But of course, in the end, there was never any money at all, and if the victim does indeed wire any type or kind of currency, it will never be sent back again, despite all of the legal action that can be taken.

## THE DIFFERENT WAYS IN WHICH THE VICTIM CAN BE LURED

Earlier in this chapter of this book, we examined some of the various ways that Social Engineering Attack can also be launched as a Threat Vector when it comes to Cybersecurity. In this section of this chapter, we take a much more detailed review as to how the victim can be further lured into a Social Engineering Attack.

1. The Bait:
   This is when the Cyberattacker lures their victim by promising to give them something that they have always wanted. In turn, the victim is then tricked into installing or clicking on something that ends up installing a malicious payload.
2. The Scareware:
   This is when the Cyberattacker hits their victim with fake threats with the primary goal being for the victim to protect themselves at all costs. A perfect example is when the Cyberattacker deploys realistic-looking banners making claims that their computer may be infected with a virus or a Trojan Horse.
3. The Pretextng:
   This is when the Cyberattacker purposely lies to their particular victim about their identity. Once this level of trust has been established, they then trick them into giving over sensitive information. The previous example of the administrative assistant perfectly describes this kind of scenario.
4. The Phishing:
   As it has been also reviewed throughout this entire book, Phishing is probably the oldest of the Cybersecurity Threat Variants, having its originations back in the early 1990s. In fact, the first victim was America Online or AOL. But now, many variations of it have taken form, which now heavily make use of Generative AI. In this case, the Cyberattacker instills a sense of urgency or plays upon their victim's curiosity. In return, they get the victim to click on a malicious link or provide private information by directing them to fake website.
5. The Spear Phishing:
   This is yet another modified form of the traditional Phishing Attack. But in this case, the victim is specifically targeted, and the Cyberattacker often takes their own time and performs extensive research well ahead of time such as studying their social media profiles and using the tools of OSINT, which was also reviewed at the beginning of this book. Finally, once the Cyberattacker knows how to manipulate their victim, they can then launch the attack, with the ultimate goal of getting information, credentials, or sensitive data.
6. The Water Holing:
   In this case, the Cyberattacker attempts to manipulate a certain, targeted group of individuals by deploying pieces of malicious payload infecting the various websites that they trust. In this regard, the Cyberattacker will target those sites that are of high value, such as banking websites, credit card account websites, or anything related in which they can potentially steal the money from their victim.

7. The Quid Pro Quo:
   In this particular instance, the Cyberattacker fakes false pretenses to their specific victim by providing them something in exchange for information or a specific action for them to take. A perfect example of this is when the Cyberattacker pretends to be someone from Microsoft tech support and then tries to convince their victim that they should enter in specific commands or download a fake piece of software that installs a piece of a malicious payload onto their device.
8. The Honey Trap:
   In this particular instance, the Cyberattacker attempts to assume the identity of an attractive person. They then engage their victim in a romantic relationship with them so that they can eventually get sensitive information from them. This is typically seen on online dating websites.
9. The Tailgating:
   In this particular instance, this is a case of a physical form of Social Engineering. With this, the Cyberattacker actually follows following an employee someone with a high level of security clearance into an office building. Because of this, the Cyberattacker is now known as the "Tailgater". As a result, the victim either inherently trusts the "Tailgater" or, out of courtesy, holds the door open for them.
10. The Vishing:
    This is now probably one of the newest forms of Social Engineering. In this regard, the Cyberattacker uses a conversation over the smartphone with their victim phone to con their victim into giving out financial or personal information or to take a certain course of action. They often change their Caller ID to "Unknown". Just with forms of Social Engineering, the Cyberattacker tries to gain the victim's trust or uses various types and kinds of fear factors to get them to give out valuable information of sorts.

## HOW NOT TO BECOME A VICTIM OF SOCIAL ENGINEERING

At this point, it is very important to keep in mind that the bottom line of Social Engineering Attacks is to provide Misinformation and Disinformation to their victim so that their vulnerable state of mind can be preyed upon so that they will almost act as if they are brainwashed and will do anything that the Cyberattacker asks them to. But, it is also very important to keep in mind as well that one can never 100% avoid from becoming a victim of Social Engineering. Rather, all one can do is ***simply mitigate the risks of happening to them.*** So in this section of this chapter, we provide some tips so that you can accomplish this very important goal.

## Pointers

1. Be Aware:
   Just like anything else in life, you have to be constantly aware of what is happening around you in both your external and internal environments. So, when it comes to a Phishing email, never click on the link in the Phishing email. Instead, manually type in the Uniform Resource Locator (also known as the "URL"). If you are still suspicious after doing this, try to do more background checking, and if you still cannot verify the website's legitimacy, the best line of defense is to avoid it altogether.
2. Use MFA:
   This is an acronym that stands for "Multifactor Authentication". In this regard, the place of business is using at least three or more authenticating mechanisms in order to fully the identity of the employee in question. This is illustrated in Figure 3.2.
3. The Password:
   If you are a business owner and still use passwords as your primary means of authentication, this is still probably your weakest link in

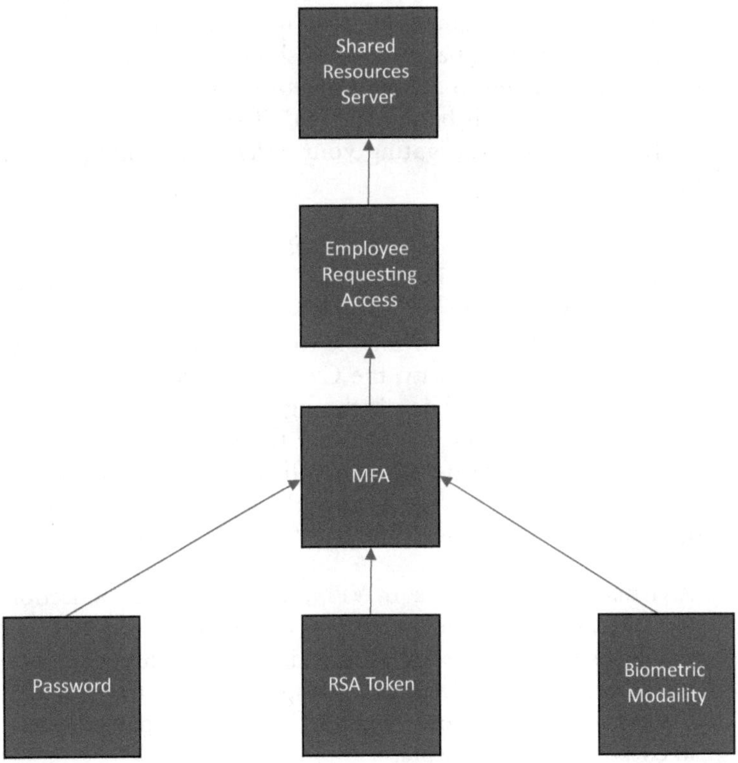


*Figure 3.2* This is an example of MFA.

the proverbial security chain. After all, the password is still a much cherished for the Cyberattacker, and employees, despite all of your best efforts, will still attempt to create and use passwords that are basically easy to remember. Therefore, you will want to make use of what is known as a "Password Manager". It can be technically defined as follows:

> A password manager is a technology tool that helps internet users create, save, manage and use passwords across different online services.
>
> *Source: https://www.techtarget.com/searchsecurity/definition/password-manager*

Probably the biggest advantage of this software package is that it can automatically create and store long and complex passwords so that your employees will not have to do this.

4. The Real World:
   It seems that ever since the COVID-19 pandemic, people have been isolated from physical contact with other people. This was especially true when the Remote Workforce came into being. But when it comes to Social Engineering, it is important to keep in mind to have physical contact based relationships as well. Of course, there are many advantages to this, but one of the biggest ones here is that you will form a much better "hunch" if somebody is actually real or not, thus further mitigating your risks of becoming a victim of Social Engineering.
5. The Wi-Fi:
   Who doesn't love to go to a local café, plug in their laptop, and get work done? Probably a lot of people enjoy doing this. But, there is one major problem with this: The Wi-Fi connection that is provided is insecure. Meaning, it is available to anybody, and even the Cyberattacker. With this insecurity, the Cyberattacker can easily hack into your wireless device and comb through all of your files in order to build up a profile about you in order to launch a subsequent Social Engineering Attack. Therefore you will want to make use of what is known as a "Virtual Private Network", also known as a "VPN" for short. A technical definition of it is as follows:

   > A virtual private network, or VPN, is an encrypted connection over the Internet from a device to a network. The encrypted connection helps ensure that sensitive data is safely transmitted. It prevents unauthorized people from eavesdropping on the traffic and allows the user to conduct work remotely. VPN technology is widely used in corporate environments.
   >
   > *Source: https://www.cisco.com/c/en/us/products/security/vpn-endpoint-security-clients/what-is-vpn.html*

Put in simpler terms, you can still connect to the Internet using public Wi-Fi, but all of your communications will take place over a second line, which is completely encrypted. Thus, your chances of being a victim of a Social Engineering Attack in this regard are greatly mitigated. Also, it is important to keep in mind that VPNs are a software application, and they can be obtained very easily and at a very low cost from an Internet Service Provider, or even a Domain Registrar, such as Namecheap and GoDaddy. This also includes your home networking equipment, such as your Router. Make sure that it is protected with a strong password, and that only you have access to it.

6. The Software:
   Whatever device you might be using, if it is a laptop or even a smartphone, make sure that you have a good Internet Security software package that is installed on it. For example, it can greatly protect your device from Malware being deployed that gets implanted from a Social Engineering Attack. Also, these kinds of software packages can also track the source of the attack, which can be used by law enforcement not only as evidence but to even track down the perpetrator as well.
7. The Safety:
   In this regard, you need to make sure that all of your devices (both hardwired and wireless) are always locked up or with you at all times. This holds true for both your personal and work-related devices.
8. The Updates:
   Making sure that all of your devices are updated with the latest software upgrades and patches, will ensure your applications and PII datasets that are stored onto them are more or less immune to the latest types and kinds of Social Engineering Attacks that are looming. So, be sure to frequently update all of your devices, or better yet, set up alerts so that you will be made aware when the latest software patches, updates, and firmware become available for you to download.
9. The Checking:
   In this regard, you will always want to do a routine check on your online banking and credit card accounts. The recommended rule of thumb is at least twice a day. It is important to keep in mind that although Social Engineering Attacks are designed to prey upon the vulnerable state of mind of the victim in question, the ultimate goal of them is to make a profit, whether it involves stealing from your banking account or using your credit card in a fraudulent scheme.

## REAL-WORLD EXAMPLES OF SOCIAL ENGINEERING ATTACKS

To show just how dangerous Social Engineering Attacks are, in this last section of this chapter, we review some of the more devastating ones that have happened.

1. The Shark Tank:
   One of the hosts of this famous show was literally conned into a $400,000 Social Engineering Attack in 2020. A Deepfake was created for their administrative assistant and from there, a Phishing email was then sent for payment related to a real estate property. Also, an email address was used that was extremely close to the real and authentic legitimate one.
2. The Toyota:
   The Toyota Boshoku Corporation, a subsidiary of Toyota became the victim of a BEC Attack back in 2019. The financial loss totaled $37 million. An employee was conned over time to make this wire transfer.
3. The Carrabus County:
   This particular county was also the victim of a BEC Attack. The financial loss totaled a loss of $ 1.7 million back in 2018. The Cyberattackers impersonated real employees and county suppliers and conned others to make a series of payments to an offshore bank account. In this case, fake but real-looking invoices were used.
4. The Ethereum Classic:
   Back in 2017, many people literally lost thousands of dollars in cryptocurrency after the website of the Ethereum Classic was hacked into. By using the concepts of Social Engineering, the Cyberattackers were able to impersonate the owners of this virtual currency project. By doing this, the domain that was used to host the website was then redirected the domain to their own server. By doing this, the Cyberattackers were then able to heist the Ethereum cryptocurrency from the victims.
5. The Ubiquiti Networks:
   This particular company, a manufacturer of various kinds and types of equipment for networking purposes, lost almost $40 million dollars, in 2015. The catalyst for this was an employee email account that was hijacked in Hong Kong. Impersonation was the Social Engineering method that was used to request the fraudulent payments.
6. The Sony Pictures:
   This is probably one of the most well-known of the Social Engineering Attacks. In this particular instance, it happened in 2014. This was one of the first ones done by a nation state threat actor, and it was carried out by Cyberattackers based in North Korea. Thousands of files, including business agreements, and PII datasets were stolen.
7. The South Carolina Department of Revenue:
   This is a Social Engineering Attack that happened back in 2012. In this particular case, the Cyberattackers literally stole thousands of credit and debit card information. This was all done via a Phishing Attack.
8. The RSA:
   This organization is deemed to be one of the world's largest security organizations, and the attack vector was a Phishing email that had a malicious payload that was attached to it. This created a covert back door for the Cyberattacker to easily penetrate into, and stay in for a long period of time.

Chapter 4

# The effects of cyberbullying on Misinformation and Disinformation

Picture a world where one falsified video can ruin someone's reputation and coordinated online harassment campaigns silence voices, while simultaneously, blurred lines between truth and lies create indistinguishable shades of gray (Figure 4.1). The current digital era presents a unique danger as cyberbullying starts to combine with Misinformation and Disinformation, creating one harmful environment.

A phenomenon that began as simple schoolyard taunts and whispered rumors has become a worldwide crisis due to internet connectivity and the harmful influence of several social media platforms. The nature of cyberbullying has evolved beyond mere teasing as it now represents a systematic harassment pattern that is propelled by both the anonymous nature and viral potential of online platforms.

Those who wish to inflict harm use misinformation, which spreads false information without intent, and disinformation, which spreads falsehoods deliberately as powerful weapons. The combination of these elements generates an ideal circumstance where online harassment extends beyond personal attacks to encompass political and societal dimensions achieving devastating effectiveness.

This chapter aims to understand the ways in which the fusion of cyberbullying and misinformation together with fast-paced AI developments transforms online harm dynamics. The explanation will cover the development of cyberbullying starting from chatroom origins to its current widespread presence in social media platforms. This chapter also covers multiple types of cyberbullying and analyzes both its psychological effects on victims and bystanders as well as its greater impact on vulnerable groups.

The goal is to examine the process through which Misinformation and Disinformation acts as tools for online harassment while generating hate-filled echo chambers that silence opposing opinions. The final section will address the emerging threat of generative AI, which will likely escalate current risks by producing deepfakes and automated harassment bots among other synthetic media formats.

This chapter also explores the complexities within our current digital landscape while providing methods to address and counteract various

DOI: 10.1201/9781003642374-4

*Figure 4.1* The evolving landscape of online harm.

harmful online activities. A comprehensive understanding of cyberbullying's origins alongside misinformation techniques and AI capabilities enables us to create a digital world that prioritizes safety and equality.

## A HISTORY OF CYBERBULLYING: FROM EARLY CHATROOMS TO THE SOCIAL MEDIA ERA

The origins of cyberbullying emerged during the internet's initial development phase, well before anyone coined the term (Figure 4.2). The early internet platforms like chatrooms and bulletin boards enabled harassment because their digital communication allowed users to remain anonymous and distant.

Text-based attacks enabled people to harm others despite the lack of visual cues and social restrictions common in direct interactions. The beginning of internet usage with its dial-up connections and text-based interfaces promoted a feeling of detachment among users. The internet enabled people to connect beyond physical boundaries while simultaneously reducing social restraints.

Online forums frequently experienced "flaming", which refers to the posting of hostile and insulting messages. The initial methods of online harassment focused on individuals who did not follow the established norms of their digital communities. The technology limitations of early online harassment set a foundation for how digital tools could be used to cause emotional distress.

Social media emergence brought about significant changes to the digital landscape. Online harassment increased alongside the broader online interaction

*Figure 4.2* A History of cyberbullying: From early chatrooms to the social media era.

possibilities created by instant messaging tools such as AOL Instant Messenger and early online forums.

The launch of social networking sites, such as MySpace alongside Facebook and Twitter, represented a significant shift. Social platforms generated unparalleled opportunities for connecting with others yet simultaneously opened up new paths for cyberbullying. People started using the term "Cyberbullying" more frequently when these platforms expanded.

The internet's increased visual connectivity led to a dramatic expansion of harassment methods. Instant content sharing combined with anonymous posting led to significantly increased harassment effects. Insults and rumors spread quickly throughout a massive audience within seconds.

Cyberbullying tactics evolved alongside these new forms of technology. No one having any type of consent to disclose sensitive personal information became a weapon that people deployed to humiliate others.

The practice of "exclusion" involved intentionally removing someone from online communities which led to their social isolation. The creation of fake profiles to post malicious content under someone else's identity heightened the confusion between reality and illusion.

Then, the emergence of multimedia content introduced a fresh aspect to the phenomenon of cyberbullying. Manipulated images and videos allowed perpetrators to share harmful content that humiliated victims across large networks.

This is also when the occurrences of revenge porn also began. It often began with couples offering or taking adult-style images of each other while in a relationship then broke up, and those images were shared among friends or online to humiliate the ex-partner.

Virality enabled rapid content distribution while amplifying harm in an exponential fashion. Certain platforms offered anonymity which permitted users to launch attacks without worrying about being held accountable. Cyberbullying developed in parallel with the changes and growth of the internet.

Online tools aimed at causing harm have evolved alongside technological developments. Today's current challenges often stem from historical developments in cyberbullying, which people must understand and study to create successful future prevention strategies.

## THE UNIVERSAL REACH OF CYBERBULLYING: NO ONE IS IMMUNE

The common misunderstanding about cyberbullying is that only young people experience it (Figure 4.3). Children and adolescents face significant risks from cyberbullying but this threat impacts people across all ages and professional levels.

The digital era ensures that everyone remains susceptible to cyberbullying. Adults quickly lose their sense of security when they face the harsh truths of online harassment.

Adults face the same bullying tactics that affect children, and these techniques leave emotional wounds that may become deeper in adults because of life's additional complexities. Online smear campaigns can threaten professional careers while manipulated images and false rumors can destroy

*Figure 4.3* The universal reach of cyberbullying: No one is immune.

personal relationships and doxing or online stalking can invade personal home security.

Telling adults to "just ignore it" or "be more resilient" overlooks how severe online harassment affects mental health and personal well-being. The internet's constant accessibility creates a perpetual threat since harassment invades private spaces to disrupt sleep patterns and generate anxiety while diminishing personal safety.

Online interactions create a situation where professional and personal lives merge together more often than before. An ill-advised post or comment has potential for rapid escalation into a public relations crisis which threatens both personal reputation and professional stability.

Online anonymity does not protect individuals who maintain a low profile from harassment when their opinions or behaviors are labeled as controversial. Internet anonymity gives people the confidence to behave in ways they would avoid during personal encounters. The combination of internet anonymity and swift information distribution creates an environment where cyberbullying can affect people regardless of their age.

The fact that cyberbullying affects individuals across all demographics requires us to adopt a complete strategy for digital security. Protecting children alone is insufficient because adults need education about online harassment risks along with necessary resources and support for their digital safety.

All age groups must develop empathy and respect to understand that online behavior leads to real consequences in the physical world. The initial step toward a secure digital community that welcomes everyone requires us to acknowledge the susceptibility of all individuals across different age groups.

## THE ANATOMY OF CYBERBULLYING: WHAT IT LOOKS LIKE AND WHO IT AFFECTS

The problem of cyberbullying exists in multiple forms that display distinct features while often delivering severe outcomes (Figure 4.4). Effective resolution of cyberbullying requires knowledge about its different manifestations and how it affects individuals and communities.

Text-based harassment represents a common category of online abuse that includes harmful actions such as sending threatening or insulting messages directly to users and posting derogatory comments on social media while spreading rumors across online forums or group chats. The internet's anonymous environment empowers users to express themselves with more extreme language and more aggressive conduct than they would use in direct personal encounters.

The widespread availability of digital media has led to visual harassment through image and video manipulation to shame victims. Plus, add in the

*Figure 4.4* The anatomy of cyberbullying: What it looks like and who it affects.

creation of deepfakes that disseminate deceptive stories along with the unauthorized sharing of private images, and the situation becomes even more dire. Groups of cyberbullies execute coordinated attacks, which allows them to exert greater impact through their online harassment efforts.

Cyberbullies may inundate social media profiles with abusive messages while they spread misinformation through coordinated campaigns and plan virtual attacks to interrupt web-based gatherings. Doxing and online stalking consist of revealing personal details about a victim, like their home address or phone number, to harass them while also tracking and harassing their internet behavior. The psychological effects of cyberbullying are typically both severe and enduring, which often results in:

- Anxiety disorders
- Depression
- Self-esteem issues
- Social withdrawal
- And more!

Online harassment that occurs consistently can generate feelings of powerlessness and exposure, which unfortunately often results in deep despair and suicidal thoughts. The phenomenon where people refrain from intervening in situations with other observers present occurs online as well because numerous witnesses choose not to act due to fear or because they expect someone else to step in.

Aggressors who engage in repeated bullying tend to become desensitized and lose their ability to empathize with others. Unfortunately, vulnerable populations are disproportionately affected.

Young people face increased vulnerability because their social abilities and emotional development remain in progress. That means persistent online harassment seriously affects their mental wellbeing. People from marginalized groups, which include LGBTQ+ individuals along with racial minorities and those with disabilities, face discrimination simply because of their identity.

The anonymity of the internet provides perpetrators with the ability to attack public figures and journalists to silence their voices and discredit their work without facing any consequences. Some attackers choose to go after big-named celebrities as well as businesses as well. The anonymity online communication methods provide allows them to feel powerful and as though any type of consequence will never find them, no matter who they choose to go after.

## MISINFORMATION AND DISINFORMATION: FUELING THE FIRE

Although the digital age enables quicker information dissemination than ever before, it simultaneously fosters environments that facilitate the spread of Misinformation and Disinformation (Figure 4.5). Weaponized digital forces enhance cyberbullying damage by transforming personal attacks into extensive online harassment operations.

The rapid distribution capabilities of social media platforms enable both unintentional misinformation and intentional disinformation to spread widely. While algorithms focus on increasing user interaction, they

*Figure 4.5* Misinformation and Disinformation: Fueling the fire.

unintentionally spread false stories because they trap users inside echo chambers by only showing them content that supports their pre-existing beliefs.

Automated profiles that simulate human behavior act as primary tools for disseminating large amounts of Misinformation and Disinformation. Programmable accounts enable high-volume postings that overwhelm social media platforms with deceptive content, which is also known as fake news.

Many social media sites lack proper fact-checking procedures, which allows false narratives to spread quickly. Users demonstrate higher likelihood of trusting and disseminating unverified information when reliable sources are not available.

The modern use of cyberbullying functions as a mechanism to suppress critical thought by targeting dissenting voices. Individuals or groups who reveal misconduct or oppose dominant stories face targeted harassment campaigns.

People and organizations face reputational harm and credibility loss when they become targets of false information campaigns. False impressions can be created through rumor spreading, evidence fabrication, or image and video manipulation.

Fake accounts serve as common tools for distributing misinformation when initiating cyberbullying campaigns. The ability to create these accounts without revealing identity makes it hard to identify who is behind the harassment activities. Dominion Voting Systems experienced cyberbullying and disinformation attacks because of false claims spread about their organization.

The impact of disinformation campaigns extends beyond the virtual world by shaping public opinion and political dialogue while also triggering violent events. False information can destroy institutional trust while weakening democratic systems and generating widespread fear and uncertainty.

Journalists and public figures face severe harm when cyberbullying combines with disinformation because they frequently become targets of harassment campaigns meant to silence them and damage their professional reputation. Recent elections demonstrated the power of disinformation to produce real-world harassment against election workers.

## GENERATIVE AI: AMPLIFYING THE THREAT

The development of generative artificial intelligence (AI) technology represents an important milestone in the evolution of cyberbullying and disinformation tactics (Figure 4.6). AI delivers many advantages, but its potential misuse creates substantial problems for digital safety.

AI-generated videos and audio recordings that convincingly imitate real individuals now display advanced capabilities with easy accessibility to

*Figure 4.6* Generative AI: Amplifying the threat.

places that could spread the information. These advanced technologies produce extremely realistic fake content that facilitates disinformation campaigns, reputation attacks, and public opinion manipulation.

The broad spectrum of AI-generated synthetic media, which includes text, images, and audio, intensifies the possibilities for deceptive practices. AI systems now possess the capacity to produce lifelike voice recordings of any individual while simultaneously fabricating deceptive news articles and online identities.

Deepfake technology's rapid production capabilities represent a considerable obstacle. It is now possible for one person or an organization to produce and spread large volumes of false content within hours, which complicates efforts to stop disinformation.

Generative AI substantially boosts the ability to impersonate others. People who never engaged in specific actions or statements in the past can be shown falsely doing so through these technologies, which damages their reputation and typically causes emotional harm.

AI-powered harassment is another growing concern. AI-powered automated harassment bots enable targeted attacks against individuals or groups. These AI-powered bots create custom insults and threats that serve to intensify the effects of cyberbullying through personalized abusive content.

Personalized harassment through AI enables attackers to customize their assaults by exploiting the particular vulnerabilities and interests of each victim. Personalized attacks through AI harassment bots make victims feel more directly targeted, which amplifies their psychological distress.

Fake news articles and social media posts created through AI distribution methods intensify online harassment campaigns by spreading disinformation.

The persuasive nature of AI-generated narratives often makes it challenging for users to tell apart actual content from fabricated material.

The ability to detect AI-generated content becomes more challenging as deep-fake technology and synthetic media improve in complexity. Detection methods today mainly depend on visual and auditory signals that are prone to manipulation and concealment.

The enormous amount of AI-created content presents a major obstacle for content moderation processes, as there are approximately 400 million terabytes of content (https://explodingtopics.com/blog/data-generated-per-day) posted daily. In terms of video, users upload over 43 million hours of videos (https://siteefy.com/how-much-data-and-content-is-created-every-day/) each day. Online services find it difficult to respond quickly enough to the fast expansion of fake content across social media platforms.

To effectively detect and mitigate generative AI risks, we as humans require novel technologies alongside new strategic approaches. The approach requires building AI-based detection systems while reinforcing content moderation protocols and advancing user media literacy.

AI usage requires careful ethical analysis because it stands as the most important consideration. AI technology development and deployment should follow principles that ensure transparency and accountability while respecting human rights.

## COMBATING CYBERBULLYING AND MISINFORMATION: STRATEGIES AND SOLUTIONS

To effectively tackle the issues of cyberbullying and misinformation, there must be a comprehensive strategy put in place that merges educational initiatives with platform responsibility, legal policy responses, and community support systems (Figure 4.7). It is essential to provide individuals with skills for evaluating online information while teaching them to detect misinformation and understand cyberbullying risks.

Educational programs need to concentrate on building critical thinking abilities alongside media literacy and responsible online conduct. Promoting active reporting and speaking up against cyberbullying among individuals helps establish a supportive environment and accountability framework.

Through bystander intervention training, individuals learn to identify cyberbullying and create appropriate methods for intervention. The emergence of deep-fakes and AI-generated misinformation demands public education on identifying and avoiding fake content.

The initiative provides instruction on identifying manipulated media while raising awareness about the risks of AI-generated deception. Online services need to develop strong content moderation systems and establish straightforward user report tools for cyberbullying and misinformation cases.

*Figure 4.7* Combating cyberbullying and misinformation: Strategies and solutions.

We need full disclosure about algorithms that control content sharing and data collection to ensure platforms face consequences for their role in spreading damaging content. A discussion needs to take place regarding social media platforms' accountability for the content distributed on their services.

Legal systems must develop clear laws which clearly define cyberbullying and online harassment, while also creating legal remedies for victims. The international scope of disinformation campaigns demands that countries work together to create strategies for effective detection and mitigation.

Social media platforms can automate content moderation and reduce human reviewer workload by using AI-driven tools designed to identify and eliminate cyberbullying and misinformation. Online communities that are safe and supportive for cyberbullying victims help people overcome feelings of isolation while giving them access to necessary resources and support.

Victims of online harassment and cyberbullying require access to mental health services and legal aid to receive proper support. Online communities should embrace empathy and respect since this approach helps stop cyberbullying, while creating digital spaces that welcome everyone.

## THE FUTURE OF DIGITAL SAFETY: A CALL TO ACT

Combating cyberbullying and misinformation requires continuous monitoring and adaptable strategies because it is an unending struggle (Figure 4.8). The evolution of technology demands corresponding advancements in our methods to protect all types of digital environments.

*Figure 4.8* The future of digital safety: A call to act.

The digital environment remains constantly evolving because new technological platforms and tactics emerge constantly. Both individuals and institutions must maintain a consistent dedication to learning and adapting in order to meet ongoing challenges.

The fight against both cyberbullying and misinformation constitutes a long-term process that requires sustained effort rather than a one-time event. Effective response to constantly changing threats requires continuous monitoring and resource allocation.

Multiple defense strategies that make up a layered approach are essential because no single solution works universally. Each person plays an essential role in creating an online environment that emphasizes safety and respect.

Responsible online behavior requires consistent practice which involves:

- Thorough information verification before sharing it with others.
- Careful attention to language communication.
- Respecting personal privacy online.

People can help create a positive online space by reporting cyberbullying and misinformation when they notice it and supporting those who suffer from online harassment.

The cultivation of digital citizenship and empathy during online interactions represents a critical priority. Creating a secure digital future requires joint efforts from individuals, communities, platforms, and policymakers.

Developing new technologies and strategies to combat cyberbullying and misinformation requires the same level of innovation as other forms of technological advancement. Investments should flow into AI detection systems, while educational resources expand and safe digital environments get established.

Our goal should be to establish a digital environment where every person feels protected and respected while having the freedom to fully engage. The significant challenges that exist do not diminish the strong basis for optimism that remains.

Through collaboration, we aim to create a digital space that offers increased safety and fairness while promoting human development. The ability of people and communities to withstand cyberbullying and misinformation highlights the power of human connection and the ongoing quest for truth. We need to acknowledge that positive online interactions outnumber negative ones, and our responsibility lies in promoting these positive exchanges.

Chapter 5

# Tools to mitigate the spread of Misinformation and Disinformation

So far in this book, we have covered the following topics:

- What Misinformation and Disinformation are all about.
- The impacts of Generative AI on Misinformation and Disinformation (with a focus on Deepfakes).
- The impacts of Social Engineering on Misinformation and Disinformation.
- The impacts of Cyberbullying on Misinformation and Disinformation.

In this final chapter of this book, we examine a theoretical model in which the spread of Misinformation and Disinformation can be mitigated.

This section of this chapter will provide an overview of what is known as the "Technology Acceptance Model", also known as "TAM". This is a model that was created in the 1980s from the standpoint of technological acceptance, but we have modified it so that it can be used in the believability of information and data.

## THE TECHNOLOGY ACCEPTANCE MODEL

This has become known as the "Technology Acceptance Model", or "TAM" for short. It simply states that the adoption of a particular IT system is dependent upon two key variables:

- The perceived Ease of Use of the System;
- The perceived Usefulness of the System.

It can be diagrammed in Figure 5.1.

So as one can see, a quick adoption of an IT system is dependent upon how the end user (in this case the Remote Worker) feels it is easy to use, and how much more productive it will make them not only in their current job, but also even in their daily lives as well.


DOI: 10.1201/9781003642374-5

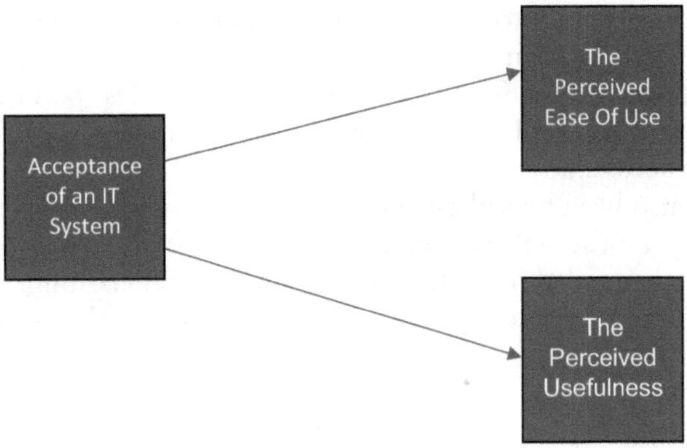


Figure 5.1 How TAM works.

It is important to note at this point that an IT system can be defined as any piece of hardware or software package that the end user either wishes or needs to adopt quickly, over a short period of time. But before we do a deep dive into the Technology Acceptance, it is first important to define what adoption really is, and some of the other major theoretical frameworks that have led up to the creation of the TAM.

## THE DEFINITION OF TECHNOLOGICAL ACCEPTANCE

Based on the literature, adoption can be technically defined as follows:

> Technological acceptance, often explored through the Technology Acceptance Model (TAM), refers to a user's willingness to use and integrate a specific technology, influenced by their perceived usefulness and ease of use.
>
> *Source: https://www.google.com/search?q=what+is+technological++acceptance*

Breaking this definition down further here are the key components of it that merit further attention:

1. There must be some sort of willingness by the end user (such as the Remote Worker) to fully adopt the IT system for use. It is important to note that this must be of free will, and it cannot be forced upon the end user. Also, the IT system must be adopted in its whole or entirety, it cannot be adopted in bits and pieces.
2. Acceptance can also be viewed as the final make or break for the IT system after it has been developed, procured, and implemented. If it

has not been adopted by free choice and in its 100% wholeness, then the entire IT system will go to an entire waste.

3. The above point is further substantiated by the last point made in the definition. After all, the bottom line is why create something if it will not be accepted?
4. It has also been hypothesized that if an IT system is adopted in its full entirety by the will of free choice, then more information and data will be demanded from it, thus pushing it to its maximum and optimal levels that are possible as set forth by the specs of the IT system.

## THE TECHNOLOGY ACCEPTANCE MODELS

As the title of this subsection implies, there actually have been three different versions of the TAM since its first inception. The first was created by Fred Davis.

1. The Technology Acceptance Model:
   This was the first model to make full usage of pure psychological variables that affect technology acceptance and out of all of the models just reviewed in the last section Theory of Reasoned Action model that forms the backbone of the TAM model. This model states that the variables of Perceived Usefulness and Perceived Ease of Use ultimately determine the adoption and usage of an IT system, with the Intention To Use (Attitude) serving as the Mediator Variable of actual system use. Further, Perceived Usefulness is also seen as being directly impacted by the Perceived Ease Of Use.
   This is illustrated in Figure 5.2.

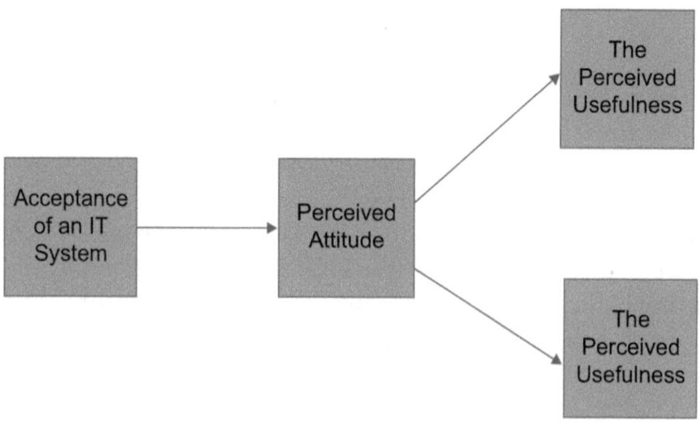


*Figure 5.2* How the 1st version of TAM works.

2. The Technology Acceptance Model (TAM2):
   This second model of TAM is a theoretical extension of the original TAM model to address the following:
   - The impacts of Social Influence and Cognitive Instrumental processes;
   - How the effects of these determinants change with increasing user experience over time with the fully adopted IT system.
3. The Unified Theory of Acceptance and Use of Technology (UTAUT):
   The UTAUT is deemed to be the third version of the original TAM model. This greatly enhanced model consists of eight new variables, which are as follows:
   1. Performance Expectancy;
   2. Effort Expectancy;
   3. Social Influence;
   4. Facilitating Conditions.
   5. Gender;
   6. Age;
   7. Voluntariness;
   8. Experience.

## THE SCIENTIFIC LIMITATIONS PRESENTED BY THE TECHNOLOGY ACCEPTANCE MODEL

Although the TAM has been in use for quite a long time (since 1985 to be exact), there have been a number of key criticisms drawn to it. Probably the biggest one has been that TAM has only been used in a controlled environment, such as that of an academic one, where primarily students are surveyed. Thus, as other researchers have pointed out, it is quite difficult to extrapolate that into a real-world setting.

The second major criticism has been that the TAM only considers the adoption of an IT system when the choice is made by free will, and not when it is mandatory. There have not been many studies with regard to the latter, and where they have been done, the results were negligible, in that Perceived Usefulness had more of an impact.

## THE CYBERSECURITY INFORMATION ACCEPTANCE MODEL

As we all know, and as it has been mentioned at the beginning of this eBook, the world of Cybersecurity is always changing, and will never seem to stop. Thus, it is quite conceivable that the TAM could play a key role in this industry in order to gauge the adoption rate of newer technologies, tools, and services as they come out by the various vendors. These can range the gamut anywhere from hardware to software applications.

But also, the world of Cybersecurity is also notoriously famous for one thing as well: The glut, or excessive amount of information and data that comes out. There is a lot of this, for example, it could be the log files that are outputted from the network security devices (thus giving rise to the phenomenon which is known as "Alert Fatigue"), and all of the news that is outputted from the major Cyber news portals that are available online.

There are other areas of this excessive information, and one of them seems to be the lack of the coherent flow of information and data from the Chief Information Security Officer (CISO) all the way down to the end user, which would include the employees that report to the CISO, external third-party suppliers, and even the internal and external key stakeholders.

Thus, we feel that the TAM could be very applicable here, and it is from the theoretical constructs that have been laid down so far, that we have formulated our own version of the TAM, and we call this the "Cybersecurity Information Acceptance Model", or also known as "CIA" for short.

Despite all of the efforts that are taken to point out to the CISO that there not only has to be a better flow of communications from the top down (starting from the C-Suite) of the entities that are external to the company, the same also applies to the internal environment as well, again a top-down approach.

Thus, one of the primary goals of the CIA Model is that it should be used as a tool to point out to the CISO, that this effective flow of communications (assuming the top-down approach) must be improved, if their organization is to survive into the future, especially when it comes to combatting the Threat Variants, where instantaneous and reliable information and data is a must to have, especially for the IT Security teams. But rather than taking a qualitative approach to this, the goal is to make it a quantitative-based one, so that the CISO can understand easily the gravity of the situation.

Our model can be illustrated in Figure 5.3.

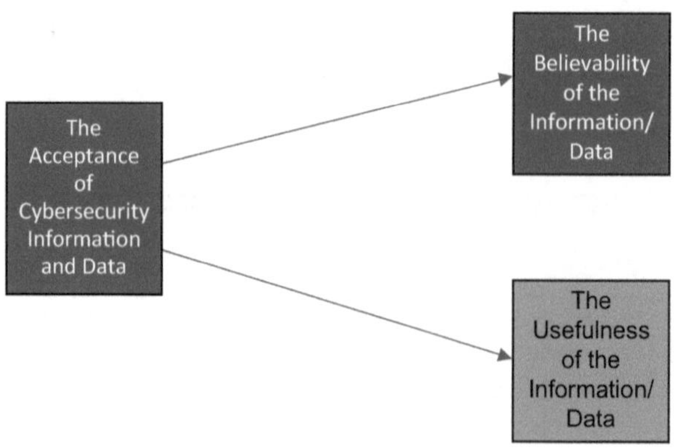


*Figure 5.3* How the 1st version of CIAM model works.

As in the same manner with the TAM, the ultimate acceptance of any information is dependent upon just how believable it is (as perceived by the end user) and how useful it can be to the end user (once again, whether it is an end user, external third party, or an employee), depending of course on how they can apply to the exact conditions that they are facing at that particular moment in time.

## A TENTATIVE SURVEY

In this subsection, we propose the constructs for a potential survey in order to gauge just how the Believability and Usefulness can impact the ultimate Acceptance of Cybersecurity information and data, which is imparted from the CISO in a top-down approach. This can also be extended to include Misinformation and Disinformation.

### For believability

1. I often become confused with all of the Cyber information and data I am receiving on a daily basis.
2. Because of the lack of clarity of the information and data that I am receiving, I make security mistakes in my professional and personal life.
3. Trying to understand the Cyber information and data that I am receiving is quite difficult.
4. I need to consult with others to discern this Cyber information and data.
5. It takes a lot of mental effort to break down the Cyber information and data that I am receiving.
6. It is easy to recover from any mistakes that I make from the Cyber information and data that I am receiving.
7. The Cyber information and data that I am receiving is hard to apply to my everyday lifestyle, whether is professional or personal.
8. The Cyber information and data that I receive produce results that I am not expecting.
9. I find it very tiresome and cumbersome to try to break down the Cyber information and data that I am receiving.
10. My daily interaction with the Cyber information and data that I am receiving is easy to deal with.
11. The Cyber information and data that I am receiving produce a more secure environment in both my personal and professional life.
12. The Cyber information and data that I am receiving guide me in performing my personal and professional tasks in a secure way.
13. Overall, I find that the Cyber information and data that I am receiving is highly believable.

### For usefulness

1. It would be difficult to perform my everyday tasks, both personally and professionally, without the Cyber information and data that I am receiving.
2. Having access to Cyber information and data gives me a greater control in helping to secure my environment.
3. Using effective Cyber information and data helps me to improve my Cyber Hygiene when I conduct my daily job tasks.
4. The Cyber information and data I am receiving address the needs for the job that I am doing.
5. Having Cyber information and data allows me to accomplish my work-related tasks in a more secure fashion.
6. Having Cyber information and data supports the mission-critical aspects of my daily job functions.
7. Having Cyber information and data makes me spend less time on other activities that may require higher levels of security.
8. Having Cyber information and data improves the level of the Cyber Hygiene effectiveness on my job.
9. Having Cyber information and data improves the quality of the work that I do on my job.
10. Having Cyber information and data increases the productivity levels of my job.
11. Having Cyber information and data makes it easier for me to do my job.
12. Overall, I find that having Cyber information and data useful for my job.

It is important to note here that although the questions being asked for the Usefulness are geared toward primarily the daily job tasks of the individual, it can also be applied to their personal lives as well.

## THE NEXT STEPS FOR THE CYBERSECURITY INFORMATION ACCEPTANCE MODEL (CIAM) AND MISINFORMATION/DISINFORMATION

Obviously, since the above survey questions are still quite tentative in nature it would have to be first pretested with other colleagues in the Cybersecurity industry. Once a point of some validation has been reached, it would then be administered to the end users of a particular Cyber company (once again, this would include the employees, other internal and external stakeholders, and external third-party suppliers).

Some sort of ranking scale would be used for each question, for example, a categorization scale of 1–10, where 10 would be highly agree and 1 would be not agree. Once the surveys have been collected and tabulated, most likely Multiple Regression Analysis will be used to analyze the results. In this manner, the CIA model can be statistically represented as follows:

$$ACI = \beta BOI + \beta UOI$$

Where:

ACI: Acceptance of Cyber Information
$\beta$BOI: Believability of Cyber Information
$\beta$UOI: Usefulness of Cyber Information

It is also quite conceivable that after the first survey has been administered and the final results tabulated, additional variables could be added to the above model, and the survey questions could be modified, deleted, or even more could be added in the end.

# Index

Pages in *italics* refer to figures.

Kolibri 360 GmbH
Ferdinand-Jühlke-Straße 7
99095 Erfurt, Deutschland
produktsicherheit@kolibri360.de